I0519289

Off Grid Living

Basic Information About Off Grid Living for Beginner

(Building a Homestead to Living Off the Land and Become Self Sufficient)

Eddie Hawkins

Published By **Cathy Nedrow**

Eddie Hawkins

All Rights Reserved

Off Grid Living: Basic Information About Off Grid Living for Beginner (Building a Homestead to Living Off the Land and Become Self Sufficient)

ISBN 978-1-9992555-9-6

Legal & Disclaimer

Table Of Contents

Chapter 1: A Path To Self-Sufficiency

Why may additionally want to someone want to apprehend a manner to be self-enough in a international that is so related?

One of the most usually taking place dreams that motivates the urge for self-sufficiency is survival preparedness. How will you ensure which you and your own family can hold to continue to exist and revel in a excessive first-rate of life while the water stops coming out of the faucet, the strength is going out for an unknown quantity of time, and supermarkets run out of meals? Now it is apparent why the motivation for this exercising is survival.

So, what exactly is self-sufficiency in recent times?

The capability to manual your very own survival without of doors help in addition to a way of existence that fosters self warranty to your capability to flourish for your non-public sources are each tendencies of self-sufficiency. Some of the important

1

prerequisites for becoming self-sufficient encompass obtaining your private meals, water, safe haven, and power.

Learning to be unbiased also can be inspired by manner of ethical and religious requirements. Some people vehemently disagree with modern governmental systems that can inspire organization malfeasance on the price of disadvantaged international citizens. People are propelled closer to more compassionate living with the aid of their choice to live without detrimental the environment, collaborating in animal cruelty, or helping human slavery.

Some human beings sincerely want for a way of existence that is more in tune with the natural international, its assets, and the folks that inhabit and deal with it. Some human beings in society discover it difficult to benefit seasonal, close by produce, and people who determine on a slower pace of lifestyles this is greater in song with the environment may additionally moreover do properly in houses

2

and neighborhoods in which like-minded human beings come collectively to promote concord and right stewardship of the land.

How to Become Self-Sufficient Mentally

The float to a self-sufficient way of life is difficult and does not take location proper away. You can increase the fortitude to preserve gaining information of latest competencies although subjects are difficult with the useful aid of adopting a strong thoughts-set to deal with your inner anxieties and uncertainties round survival.

1. Be Frugal

Adopting simplicity is taken into consideration one of the maximum important transitions from residing as a tool reliant. Compare your present property to a list of the property you really want to stay to inform the story. It can be frightening to discover ways to be self-enough in case you aren't already dwelling simply.

Only searching out what you really want can placed extra money on your pocket, lessen waste and muddle in your private home, and give you greater energy to pursue your pursuits. To help you repay debt and live inner your way, create a price range. The first diploma of liberty is to be financially independent and unattached to cloth stuff.

Keep in thoughts that the greatest riches in life are people and critiques. Adopt strategies like meditation and introspection to promote feelings of appreciation and contentment for what you have got were given. There is not anything to lose in analyzing the way to be self-sufficient in case you prevent feeling the need to encompass the materialism that society promotes.

2. Get Rid of Addiction

Even outside of managed narcotics, factors like excessive caffeine consumption, sugar intake, and screen time all bring about organic imbalances that deplete your highbrow and physical electricity. Think approximately it: if you didn't have your cellular phone, how would possibly you live to inform the tale? Detaching from socially dictated dependency in pick out of average nicely-being is a part of gaining knowledge of a manner to be self-sufficient.

three. Increase Resources and Cut Down on Waste

You may additionally additionally restrict waste and make the most of your house by using the usage of recycling, upcycling, selecting biodegradable or compostable merchandise, and using material as opposed to paper or plastic. Many topics that current Americans toss away, specifically produce that has minor blemishes, may be used again instead of finishing up in a poisonous landfill.

Even in case you do no longer understand the manner to repurpose some thing, your creative friend would possibly probable. You can also lower your carbon footprint and waste manufacturing thru manner of growing your records of crafts and survival strategies.

Consider everything as a useful resource and widely known how accurate that announcement is!

four. Attempt another time after each failure.

Nobody ever will become self-enough in a unmarried day. Being capable of help oneself is a real issue. Even while matters do not circulate as you had was hoping, reward yourself for your efforts and getting to know testimonies. You will gain the resilience you need to live independently due to this.

Chapter 2: Household Repairs

The capacity to deal with timber and do smooth carpentry responsibilities is also essential for independence. If it appears overwhelming, start with the resource of getting to know the manner to apply smooth tool because it must be, and then start jogging on easy preservation. Consider an professional mentor as a useful resource and are in search of for their help if you have get right of entry to to at the least one.

2. Create a domestic that works for you

Many people view a home as a transient residence situated among unique transient homes so that you can in the long run belong to a person else. This manner of wondering should show little hassle for keeping the residence or for maximizing its power overall performance and sustainability.

Keep in thoughts that your functionality to thrive depends on your shelter while gaining knowledge of the way to be self-sufficient. Reduce the quantity of grid strength your

7

home dreams and, if you can, include smooth, possibility energy. There are a number of starter kits available on line, and hundreds of jurisdictions offer incentives for solar power. Even when you have to spend money on a backup generator, it's miles critical to recognize that your private home will constantly have power.

You can maximize the benefits of your living situation through cultivating a garden at home, retaining water, building rainwater amassing systems, and growing family workout routines that make sustainability smooth. You can start the ones responsibilities and benefit from them even if you rent an condo.

Ask your roommates, circle of relatives people, or other human beings you live with that will help you turn out to be self-enough. A own family that cooperates flourishes as a unit. The potential to art work as a team is critical to institution survival. To benefit fulfillment, every body concerned need to be pushed to enhance the pursuits of the organization and keep each distinct chargeable for resourcefulness.

3. Establish a Homestead Near You

Homesteading is viable for you and your family when you have enough room and your private land.

Start cultivating regionally precise delicacies and heirloom sorts which have withstood the take a look at of time. Invest in chickens, goats, lambs, pigs, or exceptional animals that could produce eggs, milk, wool, and meat if you could get farm animals. To collect animal feed, you can get in touch with a close-by farmer, or you could enhance yourself-sufficiency through raising farm animals in your personal land.

Even in case you may not be shopping for cattle, consider any circle of relatives pets or animal companions you have were given already were given. Could you feed them no matter the truth that the domestic dog store closed? To make certain that everybody thrives in yourself-sufficient surroundings, begin studying approximately the dietary necessities of any non-human buddies you can have.

Preparing for Economic Uncertainty

Economic ambiguity is a truth. The monetary system will usually revel in united statesand downs, so it is critical to be ready for the possibility of a recession or unique financial problem. As a prepper, you may take measures to get prepared for economic uncertainty by way of the usage of using storing food, water, and different requirements further to unique materials, and by using way of learning survival techniques.

Here are a few suggestions at the way to be a prepper and be prepared for monetary uncertainty:

The first step is to evaluate your financial fame that allows you to discover any areas in which you could lessen your spending. This can entail lowering again on discretionary spending, such going out to eat or to the films.

To assist you preserve tune of your earnings and fees after you have were given evaluated your financial circumstance. This will help you in ensuring which you are maintaining money for a moist day and aren't spending more than you're making.

Stockpiling meals and water is one of the most important topics you could do to get equipped for monetary turmoil. You'll have a safety internet in region if you lose your hobby or cannot offer you with the cash for to buy meals manner to this. Plan to have at the least three months' worth of food and water stored up; preferably, you must have as a minimum six months.

Consider developing your very non-public food when you have the distance to collect this. This can lessen your dependency at the grocery store and let you decrease your food charges. You can expand herbs, tomatoes, and different greens in pots even on a touch balcony or patio.

Learn crucial survival capacity in an emergency, knowing the way to offer first aid, make a hearth, and purify water may be very useful. You can stay solid and live to inform the story in lots of conditions with the resource of these capabilities.

One of the high-quality strategies to be equipped for financial volatility is to create a collection of like-minded humans. This might be a hard and fast of parents that are inclined to help every other at some stage in a catastrophe, which include pals, own family, or buddies.

The Mindset of an Off-Grid Prepper

Off-grid preppers have an unbiased, resilient, and self-reliant mindset. Off-grid preppers are devoted to foremost a manner of life that depends more on their private skills and assets and plenty much less on the infrastructure and offerings furnished through the authorities.

A readiness to study is the diverse most important characteristics of the off-grid prepping attitude. Off-grid preparedness fans are typically acquiring new skills and records as a manner to increase their level of independence. This can entail coming across the way to provide their non-public power, domesticate their very non-public meals, or easy their non-public water.

A readiness to comply is a key element of the off-grid prepping mindset. Off-grid preppers are organized to alternate their plans as vital because of the reality they'll be conscious that subjects do not constantly float as deliberate. In order to perform their targets, they may be moreover willing to stay with less and give up a number of the conveniences of modern-day existence.

Off-grid preparedness fanatics are upbeat human beings. They believe in their functionality to conquer any boundaries in their path and are powerful of their capability to stay and thrive in any scenario.

Here are some tendencies you could need to increase a survivalist attitude:

Be Self-Reliant: Off-grid preppers are dedicated to important a lifestyle that is predicated upon greater on their personal talents and belongings and plenty tons much less at the infrastructure and services provided with the resource of manner of the government.

Be Resilient: People who live off the grid are mentally and emotionally prepared to cope with problems and disappointments. They are organized to persevere thru hard times because of the reality that they'll be conscious that life isn't constantly clean.

Be Independent: Off-grid preparedness enthusiasts recognize their freedom and independence. They desire the freedom to persuade impartial lives free from dependence on others.

Ability to Solve demanding conditions: Off-grid preppers excel at finding modern solutions to challenges. Even in conditions in which there are few property to be had, they could come up with progressive solutions to problems.

Be Resourceful: Off-grid preppers are able to make the maximum in their assets and are inventive. They are capable of improvise while vital and discover revolutionary methods to reuse and recycle topics.

Be Positive: Off-grid preppers have a first-rate outlook and self-self notion. They believe of their talents to conquer any obstacle of their course.

The off-grid prepping mindset is not limited to folks who intend to live absolutely off the grid. It is likewise a useful way of questioning for every person who wants to be more impartial and prepared for surprising instances.

The Three Pillars of Survival: Food, Water, Shelter

The 3 topics that humans have to have that allows you to live to tell the tale are listed above. These 3 topics need to receive top priority in a survival disaster.

Food

Humans can bypass without meals for a few weeks, but we tremendous final a few days with out water. Food is therefore the pinnacle priority in a survival emergency.

There are several alternatives for obtaining meals in a survival scenario. You can flow fishing, looking, or foraging for berries and flora in the wild. Growing your non-public food is a few different choice, however it calls for time and preparation.

If you have got were given get entry to to food, it is vital to nicely shop it to hold it from going horrible. Food may be preserved in a number of strategies, which includes freezing, drying, and canning.

16

Water

Without water, humans can handiest go through for a few days. Water is therefore the second maximum important useful aid in a survival emergency.

You can cleanse water from natural resources or accumulate rainwater further to consuming it. Water can be stored in boxes as well.

It is vital to smooth water earlier than consuming it, if you have access to it. Boiling the water, the usage of a water easy out, or the use of chemical materials to disinfect the water are all alternatives for attaining this.

Shelter

We are protected in competition to the climate, which incorporates snow, wind, and rain, with the aid of our safe haven. Additionally important to retaining us dry and heat is shelter.

You can discover a cave or a hollow tree for herbal protection. You can also assemble a secure haven, like a lean-to or a hut crafted from of debris.

Add insulation, along with leaves or branches, to do this. A fireside additionally may be brought for warmth.

You want to be prepared as a prepper to stay to tell the story in a variety of activities. Having a method for refuge, meals, and water is critical.

Chapter 3: Crafting Your Off-Grid Roadmap

The method of making a technique for sporting out your off-grid goals is referred to as growing an off-grid roadmap. This consists of evaluating your present situation, putting in place desires, and growing a technique for motion.

Assessing your current circumstance is step one on your preppers' street map to surviving off the grid. This includes determining your price range, goals, and priorities further in your skills and capabilities. What talents do you already own? What assets already do you have got got? What do your off-grid preparations aim to accomplish? Do you need a brilliant way to stay completely off the grid, or are you greater inquisitive about being able to go through a calamity for a few weeks or months?

The 2nd step is to create sensible desires. You can begin setting goals in your off-grid arrangements as soon as you've got were

19

given evaluated your present situation. Your desires want to to be time-high-quality, extensive, measurable, and express. For instance, a particular goal may be to turn out to be gifted in meals canning and preservation inner six months.

Thirdly, you ought to create a legitimate method. You'll have a bonus even as growing a step-via-step plan to make your dreams a reality when you have a realistic purpose.

Fourth, always have a look at and revise your plan as important. As a live file, your off-grid roadmap dreams non-stop assessment and updating. It is crucial to affirm that your plan continues to be relevant and feasible given the opportunity that your situation and goals may furthermore trade through the years.

Building a sustainable refuge is one of the maximum vital assets you need to do not forget as a prepper. A secure haven undertaking is one which builds a snug and regular dwelling vicinity the use of sustainable substances and production techniques. These tasks is probably as honest as building a rain barrel to seize runoff or as tough as growing a sun-powered house.

The benefits of sustainable housing tasks are severa. These obligations can reduce your dependency on governmental services, help you hold coins on electricity, and decrease your environmental effect. Additionally, sustainable shelters are regularly extra resilient and prolonged-lasting than conventional shelters, making them excellent for preparedness enthusiasts.

We must begin through developing four sustainable initiatives in this financial ruin.

Have you prepared? Let's get going!

Building Your Off-Grid Sanctuary

The process of creating an off-grid hideaway is what topics. Although it requires effort, organization, and time, it is a profitable and extremely good way to stay.

The fast-paced way of life inside the suburbs or cities often makes you need to take every week off and adventure to places with few offerings or human beings so you can spend first-class time with the useful resource of yourself, alongside aspect your mind, and on the side of your family.

In addition, residing off the grid can frequently assist you detox from the junk meals you devour, the pollutants you breathe, and the amount of strain your eyes enjoy even as looking at a pc, cellular cellphone, or television.

But with the price of town living developing, it may be hard to have the funds for those vacationer points of interest, locations, or off-the-grid places.

An off-grid safe haven can be built in quite some methods. Simple cabins, yurts, or even treehouses may be built. Hydropower, wind mills, and sun panels can all be used to deliver energy.

An ideal sanctuary must consist of more than 100 and fifty acres of land in which it can develop its very very own food and offer an area for retreat wherein human beings can studies and emerge as aware of what subjects most in lifestyles.

Materials Needed

i.   Piece of land

ii.   Shelter materials (wooden, logs, clay, and many others.)

iii.   Water series tool (rain barrels, properly, and so on.)

iv.   Energy era system (solar panels, wind turbine, hydropower, and so forth.)

v.   Food manufacturing machine (lawn, livestock, and so forth.)

vi.   Tools and components

Step-with the resource of-step Guide

i.   Find a pleasant vicinity: Think about topics just like the climate, water availability, and those nearby. Consider zoning regulations and constructing codes as nicely.

ii.   Create a technique: What form of secure haven are you planning to carry together? How will you produce each water and strength? Will you devour some thing?

iii.   Build your safe haven carefully and without a problem, as this can be your primary safe haven. Simple cabins, yurts, or maybe treehouses can be built.

iv.   Create a water supply: It is crucial for survival. You can find a close-by spring, dig a nicely, or accumulate rainwater.

v.   Installing a device for strength manufacturing: This will assist you to create your very very very own energy and reduce your reliance at the power grid. You can lease hydropower, wind strength, or solar energy.

vi.   Create a gadget for the producing of meals: It will aid you to domesticate your very own meals or boost farm animals. You can start a lawn, decorate goats, or preserve chicks.

Tiny Home Construction and Design

Tiny dwellings are growing in reputation in America for a number of amazing motives. The smaller constructing requires fewer substances to assemble, run, and keep, that could probable cause giant prolonged- and brief-term monetary financial financial savings. They would possibly surely have an effect on the resident, encouraging minimalism and a stylish alternate in mind-set and manner of existence.

Because in their duration and portability, they may be moreover quality for living off the grid. You might be wondering what you need to recognize earlier than constructing an off-grid tiny house and the manner it can dramatically beautify your sustainability.

I could likely keep you as a prepper on the same time as teaching you on all there is to

25

apprehend approximately tiny homes and their sustainability.

What off-grid device you'll need

For a tiny domestic this is honestly off the grid, you could want to invest coins on some more pieces of tool. Solar panels, generators, off-grid bathrooms, and water garage tanks are a few examples which can be and no longer using a problem obvious. Additionally wanted are a grease trap, filtration device, and greywater machine. As with most houses, you could also want to construct gutters to deflect rainfall faraway from the constructing. So, allow's talk approximately what this entail.

Powering off-grid tiny residence

Without a doubt, the most well-favored and powerful manner to strength a small off-grid home is with solar panels. They are a clean, inexperienced, sustainable deliver of renewable power, and they often offer more than sufficient power for a small house, but the particular quantity is predicated upon at the kind of humans and the form of home device applied.

Even solar systems designed particularly for tiny houses in the mean time are available. Of path, it's far important to take into account wherein to park your little residence to get the maximum daylight hours.

If you want to park within the shadow, you can get a solar device placed on a trailer. The tiny house can then be related to the sun trailer through a energy connection, which permits it to be parked in the extremely good area.

Toilet options for the Tiny House

Many human beings fear about off-grid toilet solutions in compact houses, however they may be not as difficult as they might first seem. The foremost off-grid bathroom options are composting and burning.

In a everlasting rest room with one or chambers, the quantity of which might also range depending on the emblem, natural waste is digested on net web site with out the want of chemical substances, water, a sewage tool, or a septic tank.

All composting bathrooms ought to be manually emptied even as they will be full.

Other designs are available, a few even made particularly for tiny dwellings, but the Nature's Head is my favorite because of the fact it is compact, honest to put in, and requires no protection.

In assessment, the herbal waste in incinerator toilets is burned at excessive temperatures, only a little amount of ash being left in the decrease again of, this is retained in a compartment at the bottom. They are an odorless opportunity with few safety necessities, but they're greater costly than composting options. The Superflo Macerating Toilet System is the high-quality on the American marketplace, notwithstanding the truth that there are options designed specially for small dwellings.

Rainwater collection tool

For off-grid, small-scale residing, a rainwater collection gadget is essential, however selecting the proper one for you may be difficult. As a primary step, affirm how lots water you consume. You can test your water account to appearance if you though stay off the grid. The precise amount of water your tiny house might be in a position to accumulate will then need to be calculated.

On a roof measuring 1 square meter, 1 millimeter of rain will usually result in 1 litre of water. For your specific home, use the approach below to calculate it:

Annual rainfall x roof floor area = roof catchment functionality

NB: Rainfall (in millimeter), Surface area (in rectangular metres)

The potential of your home can be taken into account while deciding on a tank length and constructing a rainwater harvesting device. To avoid clogged pipes and make sure that the water is stable to drink, a water filtration gadget is also essential.

If you need strain in your pipes or your private home cannot depend upon gravity to transport the water, you may additionally want to put in a water pump.

Grey water structures

"Greywater" is the term used to explain the wastewater from the washing device, rest room, kitchen sink, and shower. Greywater can be collected, processed, and then used in the lawn way to a greywater remedy gadget. Greywater need to in no way be dumped into lakes, creeks, or the sea to keep away from damaging our waterways.

Chapter 4: Energy-Green Home Equipment

Eco-quality insulation

LED lights

Natural lighting

Living modestly will can help you lessen your carbon footprint, however off-grid options skip a bargain similarly. The surroundings and sustainability are greater vital than ever.

Earthbag and Cob Building

Living off-grid is a first-rate in form for the green production strategies earthbag and cob. By utilizing without issues to be had substances and simple building strategies, each techniques result in robust, lengthy-lasting systems.

Earthbag Building

The method called "earthbag constructing" incorporates using earth-crammed luggage to construct partitions and specific structural factors. Earthbag walls are sturdy and robust

31

and may be constructed in quite some designs and sizes. Additionally, constructing with earthbags can be completed on a price range and with without a trouble to be had sources.

Building with earthbags is a pretty green technique that has prolonged been a contentious trouble count number number in the off-grid worldwide.

If this concept is uncommon to you, an earthbag is just a bag filled with earth. The bags are quick and quite effects piled to create homes of numerous configurations and dimensions.

You've probable visible how the military applies this principle to collect impregnable defenses toward disasters like floods. The same idea is applied in earthbag introduction to create homes which can be strong sufficient to stand as much as natural disasters, harsh weather, or even gunshots.

When entire, earthbag houses have a exceptional adobe appearance manner to plastering the stacked luggage.

Why construct with earthbags?

Cost: Earthbag creation is "dirt reasonably-priced". The bulk of traditional building substances can usually be accumulated at the development net site, removing the want for transportation or purchase in most instances.

Simplicity: Contrary to other building techniques, earthbag manufacturing just calls for a few number one competencies and data that can be imparted to others in a network.

With a few important substances and machine: A vision and a mound of earth may be converted into an amazing edifice.

Longevity & energy: Typically, the components of soil do now not harm down. A home with partitions built of earth will bear longer than one constructed of a few different.

Building an earthbag house

The first step in earthbag creation, assuming the building net web page has been cleared and leveled, is to dig a trench in which the inspiration will drift. The first layer of baggage need to be positioned forestall to forestall on top of the trench after it has been packed with spherical 12 inches of gravel.

Gravel or some one of a kind heavy mixture material should be located in the backside layers of the baggage. This provides stability in addition to permitting water to drain from the partitions.

Bags containing soil make up the subsequent layers. The strands of barbed cord which are stretched over each layer of luggage are in quick held in place via bricks.

Building within the round is one of the advised strategies for using earthbags due to the truth roundhouses are clean and noticeably durable. To hold a regular form, the muse radius is measured from a middle pole, and each layer of luggage is measured over again to verify accuracy.

Prior to constructing a door frame on top of them, it is important to install sturdy thresholds crafted from concrete or stone at entrances. To strong door and window frames to the luggage, metal or wooden anchors are positioned every few layers. Additionally, in spots at some stage in the walls wherein electric packing containers will be mounted, timber anchors are inserted among layers of bags.

Once the luggage are well piled, the ceiling is constructed. In this example, a metallic ring with extending thatched timber poles serves because of the fact the roof. In much less heat climates, heavier, insulated roofing material may be utilized in location of thatching.

Once the roofing is established place, doors, domestic home windows, and the building's façade are all installed to their frames. Starting with the wedges in between each row of bags, this concrete plaster is placed in layers until the outdoor is easy.

The equal concept underlies completing the interior of the residence. Beautiful interior finishes can be created on easy, attractive earthen plaster. It's difficult to recognize that this house's walls are built of a set of dirt sacks at the same time as you appearance inner, do now not you agree with you studied?

The last diploma of building an earthbag house is putting in area the furnishings, garage, and cabinets that make up the interior.

Cob Building

Cob is a conventional constructing approach that entails blending earthen lumps with sand, straw, and water. These structures may be utilized as houses, barns, henhouses, and distinctive kinds of systems.

Cob creation is straightforward to research, does no longer require any professional device, and makes use of sustainable sources. One shape of the earthen home, which homes almost one-zero.33 of the area's populace, is the cob residence. These constructing techniques have been hired for many years in plenty of various worldwide locations, but they've got best genuinely all began to extend to america.

Building Cob House

Asking your close by authorities if it might be viable to assemble a cob house there can be step one. "Off-grid" houses, which at one time meant houses not installation to the electrical grid, are prohibited in a few agencies.

1. Choosing Your land

You will want land with a specially stage floor in case you intend to construct a cob residence. You need to attract up a few plans for the building as soon as you've determined on a place.

Because it may be molded into organic shapes, cob is cool. Because you aren't the use of a linear constructing cloth (like timber), many cob residence thoughts contain curves, bumps, and flowing traces. The roof can be built in a in addition airy way. Others rent tarp-like materials to offer the form a more teepee-like look, on the identical time as a few use moss for the roof. Whatever you choose out, simply make certain it's suitable on your weather.

2. Preparing the constructing

Once you have a plan, maintain to the area you have were given decided on. Are there any hills or dips that want to be crammed up or moved? Of path, you can create choppy floors with cob, however it could be difficult to walk on them.

Utilizing a curler tool, compact the ground and check for any smooth spots that might ultimately sink. Cover the location with a layer of sand as fast as the development internet web site has been beaten. This will create a cute clean ground thru the use of filling in any capability choppy places.

A cob floor or poured concrete foundation can be used while building a cob house. Cob has the more benefit of being particularly long lasting after it has dried. It is unaffected thru repeated strolling on it. Want a non-slip ground? Sand want to be sprinkled on top in advance than sealing. Desire a one-of-a-type coloration? Draw it! When combining the cob, you could furthermore upload concrete colour.

In order to save you harm, it is high-quality to attend until your basis is absolutely dry earlier than on foot on it.

three. Mixing the Cob

Now that the inspiration is in region, it's time to start blending the cob in your partitions. On a huge tarp, spread 2 additives clay and 1 element sand. Lightly moisten this and step on it. Of path, use your ft. Although dust boots are elective, I favor to pass barefoot

39

just so I can feel the ground. Once the whole lot has been blended, upload a thin layer with the longest straw quantities.

After such as it, add extra. When the mixture is ready, rolling it about should now not motive it to paste to the tarp. Until the straw forms a ball that doesn't fall apart at the same time as dropped, extra straw want to be added. The wrong cob aggregate will reason your cob house to crumble, therefore this step is critical.

Chapter 5: Security Enhancements For Your Off-Grid Home

Off-grid homes want safety even extra than exclusive types of houses because of the reality it's so essential. Off-grid houses are often placed in far off regions wherein they may not have get right of entry to to utilities or public offerings. Therefore, you are responsible for your personal security and nicely being.

Your off-grid home can be made steadier in some of strategies. Some of the maximum critical consist of:

Perimeter safety: Set up a fence or gate to bar website traffic from getting into your home. You may need to install safety cameras or motion detectors.

Door and window protection: Each of your doors and windows have to have a robust lock and latch set up. You can also want to put in protection bars or window movie.

41

Lighting: Place effective lighting fixtures inside and outside of your own home. This will make it greater tough for burglars to aggregate in and deter them from breaking into your own home within the first location.

Alarms: Install a burglar alarm device or a protection monitoring gadget. If your house is accessed unlawfully, you'll be notified.

Fire protection: Place smoke and carbon monoxide detectors in each room of your house. Another alternative is to install a fireplace suppression gadget or a hearth extinguisher.

Living off the grid calls for many crucial issues, which encompass self-sufficiency in food and meals maintenance. While dwelling off the grid, you're liable for presenting your non-public food desires. This indicates which you want in an effort to expand, shop, and maintain food if you want to have sufficient to devour in the course of the twelve months.

There are numerous techniques to make certain food independence and upkeep. By cultivating your non-public food, you could do this. This interest can be done in a garden, orchard, or perhaps in pots on a balcony or patio. When you cultivate your non-public meals, you've got got manipulate over what's grown and the manner it's miles grown. You may additionally moreover choose to develop vegetation which might be suitable on your land and environment.

Additional techniques for achieving food independence and safety encompass food garage and safety. This approach of meals preservation consists of fermenting, freezing, or drying the food. Both canning and freezing permit food to be preserved for a completely long term. Fruits, veggies, and herbs can be dried to increase their shelf life. Dairy merchandise and veggies can each be preserved thru fermentation.

In this bankruptcy, I will hobby mostly on what you need to grow your personal meals as a prepper, so that you might be able to live on any unforeseen sports.

Are you prepared? Let's get began out!

Establishing an Off-Grid Food Ecosystem

A modest plot of land is usually not required to stay off the grid. You make do with what you have. Even some declare that dwelling off the grid is what people had been created to accomplish. You can start doing it proper now via the usage of your records of off-grid farming.

Knowing the way to cultivate your very very own meals is critical earlier than beginning an off-grid manner of existence. For instance, you cannot assume getting tomatoes for severa months after planting a seed within the floor. Healthy soil, regular water supply, and some smooth loving cares are required for that seed. After reading this e-book, you may have a fundamental information of while, how, or even in which to start living off the grid.

1. Locate the Ideal Location

There has been a resurgence in allotment gardening, but you do no longer need to lease a specific place whenever you want to expand your private meals. Instead, start modestly thru constructing a few raised beds or fencing off a small segment of your out of doors vegetable lawn. Get a couple packing containers out of your network garden middle to start out even greater inexpensively.

2. Prepare earlier of Season

The time period "season" refers to the durations of 12 months at the same time as the majority of fruits and veggies are at their maximum delicious and ripe. It follows that the forestall of the meals producing season is normally the maximum appropriate time to plant them. In your magazine or calendar, time desk the planting and harvesting of your plant life.

3. Mix topics up

Even in case your vegetable garden is little or you are high-quality making plans to increase food in some small bins, try and range what you plant.

Your initial sizeable harvest of green beans will seize your interest, but you will be stored worried and test masses extra from following smaller harvests of severa particular give up end result and greens throughout the only yr.

4. Examine your soil

Determine the sort of soil you have got got got before you begin your off-grid farming. Your plant life will go through if your soil is inadequate. What you want to develop determines the form of soil you need.

If you are taking a small little little bit of dust and shape it right proper into a sticky, elastic ball, you may determine whether or not the soil is clay. Particularly hard to work with is clay soil. It dreams pretty some aeration as it drains slowly and compacts short.

You have sandy soil if the floor feels and appears fragile and gritty. Despite being porous and properly aerated, it's far going to be dry, infertile, and leak water. Loam is the shape of dust that is fluffy and bureaucracy a free ball. In identical ratios, loam incorporates sand, silt, and clay. This soil blessings from effective aeration, drainage, and water and nutrient retention. Sandier loam is right for growing greens.

Scoop round inches of earth right into a mason jar to determine the type of soil you have had been given. The pot need to be virtually submerged in water. Add a teaspoon of dish detergent to aid in the separation of soil debris. Shake the jar, then leave it on my own for a day. Depending on how deep the numerous layers are, the earth will break up, displaying the overall characteristics of your soil.

Once you have got got determined the composition of your soil, you may determine whether or no longer or no longer you need to make any changes an super manner to attain the right crop output. There are some key wholesome farming techniques that you need to contain into your way of lifestyles, irrespective of the form of soil you have got got within the starting. You need to efficiently manipulate a while and electricity due to the fact living off the grid desires an entire lot of physical and highbrow strive. Cooperate with Mother Nature and delegate the time-consuming jobs to her.

five. Composting and No-Till Gardening

The success of your off-grid adventure will rely on how your lawn is installation. You want to keep what the earth has given you and return some of it to it. By permitting decaying organic count number to take a seat down at the soil's ground and redesign into new topsoil, you could increase with out tilling the ground. Immediately after that, you plant in this layer. You won't disturb the worms and bacteria, who are already hard at paintings, by means of manner of now not tilling the soil.

Weed seeds which can be underground and dormant will not sprout. Even even though you can have masses of weeds the primary couple of years if you workout no-until gardening, the longer you do it, the better your garden is probably at preserving weeds at bay. This is because of greater soil being brought to plant debris all through decomposition, which forces weed seeds deeper into the soil.

You are essentially composting at the same time as you allow the natural count number to settle. Then, you may take a step in addition. To a compost pile, you can upload your very own meals scraps, tree trimmings, eggshells, and incredible natural waste. You should hold a watch fixed in your carbon and nitrogen ratios because of the reality they'll have an impact on how brief your compost decomposes and whether or not or no longer it rots or dries up.

Animal waste is an critical aspect in composting and off-grid living.

6. Providing Irrigation to Plants

You do not want to spend all day watering plant life, however they do. You can use gravity to flow water from a nearby movement, or for a extra expert appearance, you can use irrigation drip tape or overhead irrigation. Instead of creating a pump, which even as an preference is likewise a tragedy ready to appear, it's miles maximum appropriate to art work with the slope of the floor. In order to increase your very personal meals, you need to be capable of expect troubles and obstacles and find out answers in advance than they materialize.

7. Crop Selection

Planning your fruit and vegetable garden can begin even as you're knowledgeable of the state of affairs of your soil and feature a sustainable farming technique in location, together with no-until farming.

What is the super course of movement to take first? Start through studying what grows first rate to your place. You can examine extra with the useful resource of speaking with special nearby producers or mastering the evolution of customs throughout history.

Make a desire on what you may consume subsequent. It's crucial to deliver the dishes you experience ingesting at the same time as you first start out. If you do now not, you'll lose motivation. What in case you invested an entire developing season into something, however all you ended up with had been beets and Swiss chard? What if you did no longer like beets or Swiss chard, so you ended up purchasing for kale at the shop?

It might be fine in case you started out experimenting as soon as you have got gotten the draw close of it and your flavor buds are getting acclimated to the easy meals you're cultivating. Rotating your vegetation to contain numerous meals makes enjoy. This advantages every the equilibrium of your soil and your fitness. If the worst comes, you may commonly sell it or supply it on your animals to devour.

Herbs

Herbs are important on the grounds that they may be capable of completely regulate the taste of commonplace food. Not to say that they're tasty, healthy, and smooth to expand. Having a separate herb garden is a incredible concept. Building a herb spiral is a technique for developing severa plant life in a compact place. The herb spiral is a touch spiral ramp crafted from a pile of dirt with revolving stones.

Fruits and Vegetables

Trees that undergo fruit slowly, which include fruit and nut timber, need to be among your initial vegetation. Trees need to be intentionally placed just so they will forged a substantial shadow.

Create a berry patch; it's a notable idea. Berries are perennial flowers, so that they maintain increasing. When they are dried, frozen, made into jams, jellies, and preserves, or used in pies, they taste delicious. If you placed your complete coronary heart into it, you could even create a "you choose out" garden that would can help you make a few extra money.

Vegetables are classified in line with the vitamins they require to continue to exist. To keep the soil from turning into depleted, heavy feeders, mild feeders, and heavy donors should be turned around.

There are a number of myths concerning growing grains that want to be debunked. In addition, they're as an opportunity clean to increase. Second, you do no longer require numerous land. Third, no particular machine is needed.

Once you've got got your grain seeds, plant them about 6 inches deep in a sunny vicinity. To accumulate equitable dispersion, use a seeder, which can resemble a mason jar with holes punctured within the lid. Use pruning shears or a hedge trimmer to reduce the crop (or a few factor similar) while it is ready to be harvested. The seeds must subsequent be broken unfastened from the stalks through the usage of being bashed with a stick. Finally, while located within the the front of a fan to put off the paper layer, pour the grain from one dish into every different.

A bushel of wheat can be grown on one thousand square feet of land, yielding greater or lots much less 60 pounds of grain. With that, I can bake extra or much less 34 loaves of bread.

8. Cover your produce

Some culmination and greens ought to be very well blanketed because they're more liable to frost or pests like birds and insects. Polythene can offer insect and weather safety for flowers that need to keep warmness or are at risk of frost. A first-class mesh cover will maintain creepy crawlies away although it might not offer the identical level of weather safety. If cats pose a risk in your flowers, fowl wire ought to be applied in their vicinity.

nine. Harvest the crop

When a crop is prepared to be eaten, it'll wait patiently in the ground or on the plant. If accrued earlier, some may also moreover have a superior flavor. Though it's miles essential to maintain a watch constant constant to your ripening plant life right now, you are becoming there. If you're uncertain whether or not or no longer or not a crop is ready, use your flavor buds to make the selection.

Canning, Fermentation, and Food Preservation

Through canning, fermentation, and safety, meals can be preserved sparkling for an extended time body. These techniques can be used to hold a widespread range of factors, which includes culmination, veggies, meats, and dairy merchandise.

Canning

Heat is used during the canning manner to kill probably risky microbes and save you meals spoilage. The great of meals in cans can be preserved for a very long time.

Food have to be canned the use of a strain canner or water bath canner. Additionally wanted are canning jars, lids, and jewelry.

Process meals in a strain canner as follows:

i.   Fill the strain canner with water, then heat it consistent with the producer's instructions.

ii.   Fill the canning jars with meals, permitting about an inch of location on the top of each one for headroom.

iii.   Wipe the jar rims, then positioned a lid on every one.

iv.   Use your finger to tighten the hoop on each jar to strong it.

Chapter 6: Aquaponics And Perm Culture For Sustenance

The sustainable techniques of growing food are aquaponics and permaculture. Aquaponics is a technique that combines aquaculture, the interest of elevating fish, with hydroponics, the machine of growing flora with out soil. Natural ecosystems are used as a version through the permaculture format philosophy to create self-sufficient and sustainable structures.

One can create a sustainable food manufacturing device via combining aquaponics and permaculture. In an aquaponic device, the fish waste is used to feed the plant life. The water is then wiped easy by means of way of the flowers in order that the fish can drink it all over again. As a result, a closed-loop tool is evolved with little help from the surroundings outside.

There are several strategies to mix aquaponics systems with permaculture standards. For example, permaculture strongly emphasizes the significance of biodiversity. It is vital to elevate a number of flowers and animals in an aquaponics device. By doing this, the device turns into greater resilient and is a whole lot less possibly to be attacked by using manner of manner of illnesses and pests.

A essential detail of permaculture is the use of companion planting. This includes cultivating severa plant life close to each other for mutual gain. For instance, a few flora can assist with the control of pests on one-of-a-kind flora. Companion planting additionally can be used to beautify the soil and growth harvests.

Combining aquaponics and permaculture will bring about a tool that might produce food that is reliable and sustainable. You also can combine aquaponics and permaculture by way of the use of the subsequent advice:

(i) Select some of flora and fish. The gadget turns into more resilient as a give up end result.

Companion planting is used

(ii) It is a remarkable concept to plant a number of vegetation that paintings well collectively.

(iii) Utilize natural fertilizers and insecticides. Avoid putting artificial capsules for your frame.

(vi) Recycle water and nutrients. Utilize a closed-loop system to keep assets.

(v) Develop a likely machine. Make certain your tool is easy to use and keep.

Foraging and Ethical Hunting

Foraging is the gadget of locating and collecting wild meals assets from the surroundings.

Humans have been honing this capability for masses of years way to the abundance of appropriate for ingesting vegetation, mushrooms, nuts, and berries that can be found in forests, meadows, and exquisite untamed environments.

59

Foraging no longer handiest will increase our appreciation for nature's provides but moreover strengthens our ties to the land and gives a sustainable meals deliver.

Benefits of Foraging

Numerous advantages of foraging are to be had for each the character and the surroundings.

A few maximum critical benefits of mixing foraging into your off-the-grid way of existence are listed underneath:

Sustainability: By reducing our reliance on enterprise agriculture, foraging encourages sustainable living.

Nutritional Value: Compared to their produced equivalents, wild meals regularly have advanced nutritional values.

Cost-effective: By foraging, we're capable of get food with out shelling out a fortune.

Nature Connection: Foraging offers a chance to increase a near relationship with nature.

Common Foraged Wild Foods

Although the suitable gadgets range relying on the location and season, the subsequent are a few examples of often foraged devices:

Wild Berries: Various berries, which embody blackberries, raspberries, blueberries, and strawberries, are frequently observed inside the wild at the appropriate season.

Edible Varieties: Foragers who're professional in identifying mushrooms typically search for appropriate for ingesting types like morels, chanterelles, porcini, and oyster mushrooms.

Season Nuts: Acorns, chestnuts, walnuts, and hazelnuts are only some of the seasonal nuts that can be harvested from unique trees.

Greens and Herbs: Edible vegetables and herbs may be positioned in lots of wild vegetation, which encompass dandelion greens, nettles, wild garlic, purslane, and distinct safe to consume blossoms.

Wild roots: Some wild plants have steady to devour roots, which includes the roots of burdock, wild parsnips, and wild carrots.

Seaweeds: If you stay close to the seaside, you may hunt for in shape for human intake seaweeds such nori, dulse, wakame, and kombu.

Expert foragers are seeking out cakes and healthy for human consumption lichens in addition to mushrooms from the wild.

Foraging For Truffles

Truffle searching could be a amusing and profitable sport. Truffles are significantly prized appropriate for consuming fungi that stand out for his or her one in each of a kind flavor and aroma.

They frequently increase underground alongside unique tree species and shape a symbiotic interplay with the roots.

The following want to be taken into consideration at the same time as searching out desserts:

i.   There are severa varieties of cakes, and each has a preferred habitat and a connection to a high-quality species of tree. Three famous suitable for ingesting truffle species include black desserts (Tuber melanosporum), summer time truffles (Tuber aestivum), and white cakes (Tuber magnatum).

ii.   Truffle Habitats: Specific environments, collectively with forests or wooded area areas with unique soil kinds and tree institutions, are in which desserts commonly increase.

iii.   Truffles excellent develop in certain seasons, as an example, whilst black cakes are often harvested within the winter, summer time desserts are generally located in the hotter months.

Truffle Dogs or Pigs

People also can discover it tough to differentiate the extremely good aroma of

63

cakes. Many truffle foragers use mainly knowledgeable dogs or, traditionally, pigs to find out cakes. These animals' eager feel of smell facilitates them discover desserts extra correctly.

How to Find Truffle Hotspots

Within their favored habitats, desserts are commonly placed in specific locations. Track down tips like animal hobby, disturbed soil, or formerly determined truffles.

Ethical Harvesting

When searching out muffins, it's miles vital to rent sustainable and ethical harvesting techniques. Avoid overharvesting and adverse the mycelium community that fosters truffle improvement.

Remember that discovering desserts may be tough, and achievement frequently calls for staying electricity and facts.

Finding water sourcing alternatives is becoming increasingly critical as greater humans pick to stay off the grid or in some distance flung regions. For off-grid living, there are numerous approaches to get water, each with advantages and disadvantages.

Water for off-grid housing is often received through rainwater accumulating. Rainwater from roofs and unique surfaces can be collected and saved for later use in cisterns or tanks using rainwater harvesting structures. Rainwater may be utilized for consuming, cooking, bathing, and irrigation. This useful useful resource is natural and regenerative.

Another not unusual manner to get water for off-grid living is thru drilling a properly. Wells can provide a steady supply of water even all through dry spells. However, drilling a well can be highly-priced, so it's miles crucial to affirm remarkable the water is strong to apply before the use of it.

In this financial ruin, you could have a observe in element the manner to get your very very personal water for off-grid lifestyles.

Rainwater Harvesting and Well Drilling

Rainwater harvesting is a technique for amassing rainwater and storing it for later use. Water for off-grid dwelling is commonly obtained on this technique for the reason that it's miles a sustainable and renewable useful resource. Rainwater may be used for consuming, bathing, cooking, and irrigation.

In order to build up rainwater, you can need both a fixed and storage gadget. Your roof's gutter device abilities as a collection system to direct rainwater into a maintaining tank. The storage tank may be fabricated from pretty a few substances, which include concrete, plastic, and fiberglass.

Chapter 7: Understanding The Grid

Let's kick matters off through peeling back the curtain on the fascinating global of contemporary electricity grids. You see, while you turn a transfer, a few element excellent takes vicinity backstage. It's a properly-orchestrated dance of electrons that powers your lighting fixtures, gadgets, and home device. So, how does all of it paintings?

Imagine energy as water flowing thru pipes. In a electricity grid, strength plants are much like the water sources, and the network of wires and substations is the tough plumbing device. These power plants can run on various electricity assets like coal, natural gas, nuclear, or renewable like wind and sun.

They generate energy, usually inside the form of alternating modern-day-day-day (AC). The generated power then travels via excessive-voltage transmission lines. These are just like the crucial arteries of the grid.

The motive we use excessive voltage is to reduce electricity loss for the duration of transmission. Lower voltage should result in massive electricity losses over prolonged distances. At substations, the voltage is decreased to a greater manageable degree for community distribution. It's just like the strength coming off the motorway onto smaller roads on your neighborhood.

From there, the power travels along medium-voltage distribution lines to obtain your house or commercial agency.

But, proper right here's the smart detail: electricity should now not surely glide continuously; it's miles managed via a community of switches and circuit breakers. When you switch in your lights or any system, you're essentially final a circuit. This permits power to go with the float, and voilà, your room is illuminated, your pc boots up, or your espresso maker brews your morning cup.

The grid's capability to stability the deliver and make contact with for of energy in real-time is its maximum amazing function. When you switch on a device, the grid responds by means of the usage of ramping up the power generation to fulfill the call for. The contrary takes area while you turn subjects off.

Now, proper here's wherein the plot thickens. Our present day strength grids are astonishingly complex, but they are not invulnerable. They have their Achilles' heels, and it's far critical to understand the ones vulnerabilities.

One giant vulnerability is centralized electricity generation. Most grids depend closely on a small extensive sort of large power plants. This recognition of electricity resources makes the grid prone to disruptions. A failure at a chief strength plant can bring about exquisite blackouts.

Furthermore, the ones centralized flowers are frequently positioned a long manner from metropolis facilities, making them prone to transmission losses and infrastructure damage.

Then there is the hassle of having older infrastructure. Many electricity grids spherical the arena are the usage of gadget this is well past its high. Decades of damage and tear and tear have left them more at risk of screw ups. As a stop end result, energy outages are not uncommon.

But in all likelihood the most concerning vulnerability is the grid's susceptibility to outside threats. Mother Nature can percentage quite a punch, and herbal screw ups like hurricanes, tornadoes, earthquakes, and wildfires can wreak havoc on power strains, transformers, and substations. In extreme instances, complete regions may be left with out power for prolonged periods.

Cybersecurity is every different developing trouble. In our hyper-connected global, energy grids are top desires for cyberattacks. A nicely-finished attack can also want to compromise the grid's manage systems, essential to huge chaos and outages.

So, why does this rely to you? Well, it's miles vital to understand that our current-day way of existence is primarily based carefully on a device it actually isn't infallible. The comfort of having power at your beck and contact may be disrupted with the useful resource of a myriad of things. Understanding the vulnerabilities and boundaries of centralized energy systems is step one in getting ready for a destiny in which the grid won't be as reliable as it's far today.

This isn't always about spreading fear or doubt; it is approximately being sensible and proactive. When what can pass wrong, you're in a higher feature to take control and make sure your personal nicely-being. As we assignment deeper into the world of No Grid Survival, you'll find out that it's miles now not about awaiting the worst to reveal up; it is about embracing the know-how and competencies to stand strong, irrespective of what disturbing situations come your way.

Now that we have explored the inner workings of the electricity grid, permit's take a higher examine the capability pitfalls of relying on it. Understanding those dangers and vulnerabilities is critical for making informed selections about a way to put together for grid outages.

One of the large dangers is the grid's susceptibility to natural failures. In areas

71

susceptible to hurricanes, tornadoes, or earthquakes, the strength grid is often a casualty. Strong winds can topple transmission strains and damage substations, on the equal time as earthquakes can purpose floor moves that disrupt underground electricity cables. In such situations, being without electricity for days or perhaps weeks is a very real possibility.

Additionally, immoderate weather sports, like warmness waves or bloodless snaps, can pressure the grid. During a scorching summer season, air conditioners run non-prevent, putting superb pressure at the grid. Similarly, frigid winters bring about a surge in heating needs. If the grid can not address the weight, it may result in rolling blackouts or prolonged power outages.

Cyberattacks are every distinctive concerning danger. In our generation-pushed international, power grid manage systems are excessive objectives for hackers. Disrupting those structures can bring about huge-scale outages and even compromise the steadiness of an entire location. It's a reminder that the grid's reliance on generation additionally makes it vulnerable to virtual threats.

Power grid vulnerabilities are not honestly limited to technical issues. Inadequate safety and an getting older infrastructure can result in device screw ups. When transformers, circuit breakers, or strength traces break down, they are able to disrupt the deliver of power, causing blackouts.

Now, allow's recall the actual-international affects of electricity outages. Beyond the preliminary inconvenience of sitting inside the dark or losing get proper of access to in your favored digital devices, there are broader effects which could affect every day lifestyles and society as a whole.

First and essential, energy outages disrupt essential offerings. Hospitals, emergency offerings, and verbal exchange networks rely carefully on energy. During an outage, the operation of scientific device, emergency reaction structures, or even basic conversation may be compromised. Lives are put at chance, and emergency situations emerge as even more difficult to manipulate.

Businesses additionally take a success all through strength outages. The loss of capability to behavior transactions, maintain data structures, or keep the lighting on can bring about financial losses. Moreover, for some businesses, energy outages can bring about spoiled stock, terrible the deliver chain.

Education is some different location stricken by grid screw ups. Schools and universities depend upon energy for lighting fixtures, heating, and era for education. When the energy goes out, college college students skip over treasured analyzing time, and it may disrupt the instructional calendar.

Chapter 8: Preparing For A Grid-Down Scenario

Alright, buddy, proper here's in which the rubber meets the road. We've stated the grid's vulnerabilities, and also you might be questioning, "What can I do approximately it?" Well, my friend, this chapter is all approximately helping you solution that question. It's about assessing your non-public readiness for a grid-down state of affairs and figuring out in which you may want to level up.

So, first matters first, let's determine out in that you stand right now. We're not right here to decide; we're here to help you get higher organized for some element comes your way. Start thru taking an first-rate, difficult have a take a look at your cutting-edge scenario. Think approximately the necessities - food, water, safe haven, and strength.

Look around your own home. How lengthy should you continue to exist without jogging to the grocery save? A few days, consistent

75

with week, or more? Check your water supply. Do you have were given sufficient smooth eating water to ultimate you and your circle of relatives? How's your steady haven? Do you've got got a backup heating system for those bloodless wintry climate nights, or a way to maintain cool within the warmth of summer season?

And speaking of summer season, what approximately strength? What's your plan if the air conditioner or fans flow silent at some point of a heatwave? Or if the heater might not kick in at some point of a iciness typhoon? These are the actual-existence situations we are thinking about right right here.

Now, do no longer get me incorrect; I'm not pronouncing you want to show your house right into a doomsday bunker. What we are aiming for is realistic preparedness. We're speaking approximately having a stash of non-perishable food, a few extra water, a few essential substances, and a backup strength supply. It's approximately being prepared for not unusual disruptions with out going to extremes.

Chances are, as you decide your contemporary readiness, you may spot a few gaps. Maybe your meals elements are going for walks low, or you've got by no means idea approximately what you may do if the electricity went out for an extended duration. That's all proper; this is why we're here.

Take a pocket book and jot down the ones regions wherein you could use a boost. It is probably as easy as getting some more flashlights and batteries, or it may be more involved, like putting in a number one off-grid power supply. Your list may be unique for your situation, so make it your personal.

Now, some of these obligations could in all likelihood appear a piece daunting. That's k too. Rome wasn't constructed in an afternoon, and you do now not want to end up a prepper in a single day. Think about your rate range, your abilities, and your to be had region. What can you realistically gain inside

77

the brief time period, and what is probably a extra extended undertaking?

Here's the kicker: once you have got got recognized your gaps, you're well to your manner to turning into higher prepared. It's all about taking that first step and making improvement. Remember, no man or woman starts as an expert. We all study and increase as we float.

Let's shift gears now and dive into the nitty-gritty of what you'll need to stay to tell the story and thrive while the grid is down. We're speakme approximately the requirements, the stuff that can make all the difference while the lights exit.

Alright, allow's start with the resource of list the essential necessities. These are the subjects with a view to preserve you stable, cushty, and nicely-fed within the course of a power outage.

1.   Food: You're gonna want sustenance, my friend. Stock up on non-perishable food

like canned objects, dried culmination, nuts, and rice. Don't forget about the basics: salt, sugar, and a few cooking oil. And if you're feeling adventurous, you can even strive your hand at canning or dehydrating your very own food.

2.   Water: Water is life, no question approximately it. You'll want enough smooth consuming water to closing you and your own family for at least some days. A wonderful rule of thumb is one gallon steady with man or woman in step with day. You can hold it in easy bins or spend money on a first-rate water clear out for renewable water assets.

3.   Light: When the lighting go out, you could need a way to peer. Flashlights, headlamps, and candles are your satisfactory pals right right here. Make sure you have got extra batteries for the ones flashlights. You can also find out sun-powered or hand-cranked lighting for prolonged-term answers.

4.   Warmth: Depending on in that you stay, retaining warmness might be a actual

undertaking with out power. Blankets, warmth apparel, and even a exquisite antique college timber-burning variety or transportable heater may be a sport-changer.

five. First Aid: Accidents take region, and medical emergencies do now not take a vacation throughout electricity outages. A nicely-stocked first-useful useful resource package is vital. Include bandages, antiseptics, drug remedies, and any private medicinal tablets you could want.

6. Communication: Staying in contact with your loved ones is vital. A battery-operated or hand-cranked radio can keep you up to date at the extremely-modern-day statistics and weather. And keep in mind a backup electricity supply on your cell phone.

Now, those are surely the basics, but they may be a notable location to begin. Your private state of affairs might also require more devices. For example, when you have toddlers, you may need toddler materials. If you have got got pets, don't forget their food and components.

Now, permit's talk method. How do you circulate approximately acquiring and storing those forms of requirements? Here's the lowdown.

Acquiring Supplies:

1.   Plan your buying wisely. Grab a few greater items on every occasion you go to the store, and gradually boom your stash. This way, you can not break the bank in a unmarried pass.

2.   Keep a be careful for sales and discounts. Non-perishable ingredients often bypass on sale, so inventory up while the prices are right.

three. Consider shopping for in bulk. It's regularly greater rate-powerful and decreases packaging waste.

4. Don't overlook to rotate your components. Use what you keep, and update it frequently to ensure freshness.

Storing Resources:

1. Store food and water in a fab, dry, and darkish vicinity. Avoid excessive temperatures, like a storage within the summer time, which could break your factors.

2. Label your devices with their expiration dates and use-thru manner of dates. This allows you preserve song and ensures you use the oldest devices first.

three. Organize your materials in a way that makes revel in to you. You do no longer need to be rummaging inside the dark finally of an outage.

four. Keep your vital documents in a water-resistant, fireplace-resistant field. This consists of important workplace paintings, identity, and personal information five. And remember, my friend, that your survival package deal have to be with out problems accessible. You do now not need to play disguise and are looking for for at the side of your flashlight in the route of a blackout.

Now, permit's communicate approximately a activity plan. Once you realize in that you need to decorate your readiness, make a listing of movement objects. Break it down into possible steps. Maybe it's miles as easy as deciding on up a further case of bottled water the following time you're at the store. Or possibly it is coming across solar panels for your private home. Whatever it's far, write it down and make it take location.

Here's a seasoned tip: contain your own family. Preparedness is a group attempt. Talk in your own family, talk your plan, and get them on board. When everybody's on the equal net web page, it makes coping with an surprising situation a whole lot smoother.

Chapter 9: Sustainable Living And Off-Grid Solutions

Now that we have had been given our essential substances and assets covered up, it is time to cope with taken into consideration one of the maximum critical disturbing situations in living off the grid: strength. The strength grid isn't going to be there to turn the switch, so we have were given have been given to discover alternatives. Let's take a deep dive into some of the most famous off-grid power solutions.

Solar Power: It's like harnessing the power of the solar. Solar panels, generally hooked up on rooftops or in sunny areas, capture sunlight hours and convert it into power. This is a high-quality opportunity for sunny areas, and it can energy your lights, domestic gadget, and further. There are also transportable sun panels for individuals who want to live cell.

Wind Power: If you have got were given a bit of land or open space, wind generators might be your jam. They entice the wind's kinetic strength and redecorate it into strength. Wind strength is a reliable desire if you live in a windy region, and it could provide a constant deliver of strength.

Hydroelectric Power: This one's for oldsters near flowing water assets like rivers or streams. Hydroelectric turbines capture the power of moving water and flip it into power. It's a easy and reliable supply, furnished you have got got get proper of get right of entry to to to a water source with the right conditions.

So, you have picked your off-grid energy solution, however how do you located it up and preserve it on foot without problems? Here's your crash direction.

Solar Power Setup and Maintenance:

Install your sun panels in an unshaded area that receives the maximum daylight at a few stage within the day.

Connect your panels to a fee controller, which prevents overcharging of batteries.

Use deep-cycle batteries to store more strength generated all through the day for use at night time time.

Connect your batteries to an inverter, which converts the stored energy into usable AC energy for your private home.

To hold your solar system, keep the panels clean to maximise their overall performance. Check the connections often, and replace batteries whilst their capability diminishes. Over time, you can need to update inverter and rate controller components.

Wind Power Setup and Maintenance:

Ensure your wind turbine is installation in an area with a ordinary and unobstructed wind drift.

Install a price controller to save you overcharging the batteries.

Connect deep-cycle batteries to preserve strength generated through the turbine.

Use an inverter to transform saved strength into AC strength for your property.

Maintaining a wind electricity gadget involves checking the blades for damage, lubricating shifting factors, and ensuring that the tower remains strong. Regular inspections and preventive upkeep will preserve your wind turbine in top shape.

Hydroelectric Power Setup and Maintenance:

Set up your hydroelectric generator in a flowing water deliver, making sure it's far well anchored and submerged.

Use a price controller and deep-cycle batteries to hold generated strength.

Connect an inverter to transform stored power into AC electricity.

For preservation, preserve the generator's intake easy of debris, and often investigate and lubricate transferring components.

Ensure that the connection some of the generator and your electric machine is stable.

Remember, at the same time as those structures can offer dependable off-grid power, they also require ordinary protection. It's a bit like looking after a vehicle; the better you maintain it, the longer it'll serve you.

Water, the elixir of life. When the grid is down, getting access to clean water is non-negotiable. Let's have a look at how to gather, purify, and conserve water off the grid.

Water Collection:

Rainwater harvesting is a exquisite off-grid answer. Set up rain barrels or a larger cistern to capture rainwater out of your roof. The water can then be filtered and used for ingesting, cooking, and hygiene.

Wells are some different desire in case you're in an area with a excessive water desk. A properly can provide a regular supply of smooth water for your circle of relatives.

Water Purification:

1. Filtration structures are important for putting off impurities from accrued water. Invest in a superb water clear out that can dispose of bacteria, viruses, and other contaminants.

2. Boiling water is a tried-and-real technique. Heat water to a rolling boil for a few minutes to kill harmful microorganisms.

Water Conservation:

i. Install low-waft furnishings in your own home to lessen water usage.

ii. Collect and reuse "graywater" from sinks and showers for responsibilities like watering plant life.

iii. Fix any leaks on your plumbing proper away to avoid dropping water.

Now, permit's communicate about food, a cornerstone of survival and self-sufficiency. Living off the grid manner taking more manage over what you devour and the way you control waste.

Sustainable Food Production:

i.   Start a garden: If you have a few out of doors vicinity, a garden is a exquisite manner to increase your non-public greens and herbs. You also can hold in thoughts fruit timber and berry timber for a extra prolonged food deliver.

ii.   Raise outdoor chickens: Chickens are like little food factories that produce eggs and might even offer meat if wanted.

iii.   Explore aquaponics: It's a device that mixes fish farming with hydroponics. The fish waste presents vitamins for developing vegetation, developing a closed-loop meals production system.

Food Storage:

i.   Canning and maintaining: Learn the way to can and hold your garden's bounty to experience sparkling food three hundred and sixty five days-spherical.

ii.   Root cellars: If you've got got have been given the gap, a root cellar can provide cool, humid situations that keep certain additives glowing for months.

iii.   Dry items: Stock up on non-perishable staples like rice, pasta, and dried beans. Vacuum-sealed bags can help increase their shelf existence.

Waste Management:

i.   Composting: Reduce meals waste by way of the use of way of beginning a compost pile. Compost can growth your garden soil and decrease your ecological footprint.

ii.   Recycling: Even off the grid, it's miles critical to recycle substances whilst feasible. Set up a recycling station to kind and manage waste.

iii.   Responsible disposal: For materials that can not be composted or recycled, find out accountable disposal techniques, together with a composting rest room or a nicely-controlled septic tool.

Living off the grid might now not suggest sacrificing a numerous and nutritious food plan. It technique being more aware about what you eat and the manner you produce it. With sustainable food production and storage, you may revel in glowing, wholesome meals even inside the absence of a grocery preserve. And responsible waste control ensures you depart a minimal impact at the environment.

So, there you've got it, the nuts and bolts of off-grid living with regards to strength, water, food, and waste. It's all approximately being creative, self-reliant, and making picks that align with a sustainable lifestyle. With the proper understanding and a bit of elbow grease, you may thrive off the grid and experience the peace of mind that includes being prepared.

Chapter 10: Building Community And Resilience

Building a sturdy, supportive network is essential in a international without the grid. In this sort of scenario, forming a network assist network may be a lifeline in a catastrophe. This network isn't always pretty much being extraordinary alongside your buddies; it's miles about creating a safety net and a shared imaginative and prescient for resilience.

Imagine your energy is out, your sources are going for walks low, and also you need crucial assist, whether or not it is due to a medical emergency, the need for assist with upkeep, or simply the comfort of companionship in some unspecified time within the destiny of a tough time. In a community that looks out for each special, the ones worrying conditions come to be lots extra attainable.

When you form robust connections together with your pals, you create a community of assist. You can share assets, statistics, and competencies, leaning on every specific sooner or later of tough times and celebrating collectively at the same time as subjects are going nicely. This collaborative spirit is the muse of resilience.

Now, permit's communicate approximately the advantages of running together in a grid-down state of affairs. It's greater than simply the first-class and comfortable-and-fuzzy feeling of network; it's miles about practicality.

Resource sharing is a huge advantage of an interconnected network. By pooling resources, you could trade and barter, ensuring every body has what they need. For example, if you have a surplus of garden produce, even as your neighbor has a further of firewood, you may trade items, making sure everybody's nicely-being.

Different people bring particular capabilities to the table. For example, a person might be professional in carpentry, even as a few other is a grasp gardener. By sharing records and competencies, the community as a whole will become greater self-sufficient. In a catastrophe, this diversity can be a recreation-changer.

Safety and safety additionally enhance in a close to-knit community. Neighbors searching out for each incredible can deter crime and reply rapid to emergencies.

During hard times, emotional useful aid will become beneficial. Having someone to talk to, percentage tales with, or absolutely provide a helping hand should make a international of distinction to your mental and emotional nicely-being.

It's essential to start building these connections now, earlier than you really want them. The stronger your community ties, the greater strong your manual network can be at the same time as the grid falters.

Community individuals proudly proudly owning a large variety of competencies and expertise is a treasured asset at the same time as striving for self-sufficiency in a grid-down scenario.

While you can have pals professional in cooking or gardening, thinking about what different important capabilities may want to benefit your community is important.

Medical competencies are paramount, especially having someone with clinical education or perhaps primary first-resource abilities. Organizing network first-useful resource and CPR instructions can maintain lives.

Carpentry and building talents make certain that everybody in your network has a stable and snug location to live. It's a crucial expertise almost about refuge and infrastructure.

Food production, which incorporates gardening, farming, and food protection, is some different critical information. The extra community participants concerned, the better your food safety.

Mechanical and electric powered powered repair abilties are to be had on hand whilst equipment and device ruin down. Having someone who can restore this stuff can be treasured. Communication and management abilities can maintain the community organized and focused throughout difficult times.

Encouraging the development of those and certainly one of a type capabilities internal your community is vital. Host workshops, training, and capability-sharing sessions to decorate your network's functionality set. This no longer pleasant fosters self-sufficiency however also empowers your community with a revel in of resilience.

Diversity within a community is not pretty a lot notable backgrounds; it's also about various skills gadgets. The greater skills you have got had been given inside your community, the better prepared you're for any state of affairs.

A various skill set enables create a self-enough community. You're not reliant on outdoor resources for vital offerings. With a number of abilities, your network can remedy issues creatively at the equal time as traumatic conditions arise. A numerous network is extra flexible, capable of adapting to converting events.

Knowledge sharing isn't just about the winning; it is about developing a legacy of self-sufficiency for future generations. So, whilst you're considering your network, bear in mind the severa know-how devices that can be introduced to the table.

Encourage analyzing and sharing, and include the rate of a nicely-rounded, succesful network. Together, you may be higher organized to climate the storms that lifestyles may throw your way.

Chapter 11: Thriving In A Grid-Independent Future

As we journey further right into a worldwide without traditional power grids, we want to include the version approach and discover ways to not without a doubt continue to exist however thrive in this new reality. It's time to have an terrific time the first-rate achievements and resilience of human beings and agencies in the face of high-quality demanding situations.

Adaptation is the call of the sport on the subject of thriving in a grid-impartial future. It's approximately embracing exchange, getting to know from enjoy, and locating cutting-edge answers to disturbing situations. So, how are we able to navigate this technique and emerge now not truly unscathed however higher for it?

The first step is a shift in mind-set. Rather than resisting alternate or craving for the vintage techniques, we want to actually be given that our lives can be considered

considered one of a kind, and that is ideal enough. Change is a regular in life, and in this submit-grid global, it is the new normal. Acceptance is the primary key to variant.

Adaptation furthermore includes a willingness to observe and innovate. We want to discover new era, techniques, and techniques for residing off the grid. This is a time for experimenting, for attempting new matters, and for being open to failure as a stepping stone to success.

Resilience is the backbone of model. It's the functionality to get higher from adversity, to stand as much as worrying conditions, and to persevere. Resilience isn't always approximately being impervious to problem but approximately growing the energy to undergo and thrive regardless of it.

Our companies are important to version. The greater we paintings collectively, percentage statistics, and assist every other, the better we're able to adapt to this new manner of life. In many ways, this grid-independent destiny is predicated at the power of our bonds.

Along the manner, recall to rejoice your achievements, regardless of how small. Overcoming worrying conditions, gaining knowledge of new talents, and reaching sustainability milestones are well worth acknowledging. Celebration fuels motivation and maintains the spirit excessive.

In the face of giant demanding situations, human beings and groups have showed top notch resilience and adaptability. Their reminiscences are honestly worth celebrating, as they offer perception for everybody going thru a grid-impartial destiny.

In every community, there are nearby heroes who've lengthy gone above and past to make certain their buddies' well-being. These are the parents who've organized community gardens, shared assets, and furnished their capabilities and records freely. They are the spine of resilience.

The grid-impartial destiny has sparked innovation. Entrepreneurs have advanced new generation and merchandise, from green sun systems to sustainable farming techniques. These innovators are not handiest shaping the destiny however furthermore providing answers for others.

Knowledge is strength, and those who've taken at the position of educators and mentors in their communities have empowered others to thrive. Whether it is coaching sustainable farming or sharing DIY power answers, the ones humans are the torchbearers of resilience.

Entire businesses have embraced the spirit of collaboration, growing networks of guide that supply a boost to their shared capability to evolve. Whether it's miles a community appearance in advance to safety or a food co-op for sustainability, these organizations exemplify the strength of group spirit.

Beyond nearby reminiscences, international examples of resilience and version provide choice and concept. From countries transitioning to renewable strength to companies reclaiming their water assets, those examples display that thriving in a grid-impartial destiny is not best feasible however taking location right now.

While model is important, we need to additionally set our points of interest on a sustainable and green future put up-grid reliance. It's time to inspire accountable useful resource control and offer steerage on extended-time period sustainability.

Living in a grid-unbiased destiny way adopting a way of life that not only enables your properly-being however also protects the planet. It's about finding the stability among self-sufficiency and eco-friendliness. So, how do we encourage and embody this sustainable manner of existence?

Renewable strength property like solar, wind, and hydroelectric power are the spine of a sustainable grid-impartial future. By

103

harnessing these assets, we reduce our carbon footprint and reliance on fossil fuels.

Sustainability includes using assets effectively. Whether it's far water, power, or food, we must avoid waste and make the maximum of what we've got got. This no longer exceptional saves assets however additionally saves cash.

Sustainable manufacturing strategies and substances are crucial for minimizing the environmental effect of your property. Consider power-inexperienced designs, herbal insulation, and the use of recycled or locally-sourced materials.

Reducing our carbon footprint moreover technique rethinking how we pass. Electric and hybrid cars, biking, and public transportation can be greater inexperienced options than conventional cars. Carpooling and walking from home also can contribute to sustainability.

Sustainability includes responsible waste control. Composting, recycling, and decreasing single-use plastics are all steps inside the proper course. Reducing waste no longer best advantages the environment however additionally conserves sources.

Sustainability isn't pretty a good deal making eco-friendly options in recent times; it is approximately questioning lengthy-term and being accountable stewards of our sources. Long-term sustainability includes the conservation of natural property. This consists of coping with water as it should be, defensive forests and inexperienced regions, and maintaining biodiversity.

Sustainability is intently tied to decreasing our carbon footprint. This way now not nice the usage of renewable energy however moreover being conscious of the strength we use, minimizing waste, and supporting inexperienced merchandise and agencies.

Building a sustainable destiny is predicated on schooling and raising hobby. Encouraging network people to understand the importance of sustainability and the environmental impact in their alternatives can stress powerful change.

Long-term sustainability moreover includes advocating for and assisting rules that defend the environment. This can also additionally embody lobbying for easy energy obligations, conservation efforts, and sustainable agricultural practices.

Sustainability calls for responsible consumption. It manner being aware of what we buy, wherein it comes from, and its environmental effect. Supporting neighborhood and sustainable products is a step within the proper direction.

Thriving in a grid-independent destiny isn't tremendous feasible however may be especially profitable. It's a adventure of model, resilience, and embracing sustainable residing.

While demanding situations lie earlier, the stories of these who have already released into this path provide notion and choice. With the right mind-set and a strength of will to sustainability, we are able to assemble a future that isn't always exceptional grid-unbiased however moreover environmentally accountable and resilient.

Chapter 12: Solar Basics And Fundamentals

1.1 Introduction to Solar Energy

Solar strength has been harnessed and used by people for lots of years. From the historic Greeks and Romans the use of passive sun format in their structure to greater present day enhancements in photovoltaic era, solar electricity has accomplished a big feature inside the development of sustainable and renewable energy answers.

The importance of sun energy inside the cutting-edge-day global can't be overstated. As the worldwide name for for electricity maintains to growth, the need for smooth, renewable belongings of power has turn out to be an increasing number of important. Solar power offers a truely infinite deliver of energy that is both environmentally excellent and economically viable. By harnessing the energy of the solar, we are able to reduce our dependence on fossil fuels, decrease greenhouse fuel emissions, and sell electricity independence.

Solar power has a full-size shape of programs, from residential rooftop installations to software-scale solar farms. In addition to generating power, solar strength additionally may be used for water heating, area heating, or maybe cooling in a few cases. Furthermore, sun-powered gadgets, together with solar lanterns and portable chargers, have emerge as increasingly well-known, offering essential energy offerings in off-grid or some distance flung regions.

The improvements in sun energy generation have made it extra accessible and much less highly-priced than ever earlier than. With non-forestall research and improvement, sun strength has the functionality to end up a large contributor to our international strength mix, paving the manner for a more sustainable and cleanser future. This financial ruin goals to introduce the basics of sun electricity, together with the conversion system, and the way solar panels are made.

1.2 Solar Energy Conversion Process

The solar energy conversion system includes taking photographs sunlight and converting it into usable energy. This is finished through a phenomenon referred to as the photovoltaic (PV) impact. The PV impact is the machine via manner of which sure substances, known as semiconductors, can generate an electric powered cutting-edge-day when uncovered to sunlight hours.

Fig 1.1

A solar cellular is the critical unit chargeable for this conversion system. The most common material carried out in solar cells is silicon, that may be a semiconductor. A sun cell is usually composed of layers of silicon – one layer is doped with impurities to create an excess of electrons (known as an n-kind layer), while the possibility layer is doped to create a deficit of electrons (known as a p-kind layer). When those layers are added collectively, an electric powered powered area is fashioned on the junction amongst them, growing a vicinity referred to as the depletion location.

When daylight, composed of particles known as photons, hits the solar cellular, a few photons are absorbed thru the semiconductor material. The power from those absorbed photons is transferred to the electrons in the silicon atoms, causing them to break free from their atomic bonds. These free electrons are then driven with the useful resource of the electric area closer to the n-kind layer, at the equal time because the "holes" they go away within the back of include pushed toward the p-type layer.

Fig 1.2

By attaching steel contacts to each layers of the sun mobile, an outside electric circuit is created. When the free electrons go with the float via this circuit, an electric powered present day is generated. This direct modern-day-day (DC) can then be used to electricity electric gadgets, or it can be converted into alternating current (AC) the usage of an inverter, making it suitable to be used in houses and companies.

1.Three How Solar Panels Are Made?

Fig 1.Three

Solar panels are crafted from a couple of sun cells related collectively in series or parallel configurations to deliver a better voltage or cutting-edge output. The blended output of the sun cells in a panel bureaucracy the idea of a photovoltaic (PV) module. PV modules can then be linked together to form a solar array, capable of generating a considerable amount of energy to satisfy severa strength desires.

In the following phase we can communicate the sure manner of manufacturing sun panels from raw silica.

1.Four Solar Panel Manufacturing Process:

Solar cells, generally made from silicon, are the essential constructing blocks of a photovoltaic sun panel. They convert daylight without delay into strength. Here's a primary outline of approaches conventional silicon-primarily based absolutely sun cells are made:

Fig 1.Four

Image   Credit: https://www.Solarreviews.Com/

Fig 1.Five

1.   Purifying Silicon:

Silicon is determined in nature within the form of silicon dioxide (like some varieties of sand and quartz). To extract herbal silicon, the silicon dioxide is heated in a discount furnace with carbon.

The quit stop result is metallurgical-grade silicon, that is further diffused to electronics-grade silicon the use of more than one rounds of purification.

2. Making Monocrystalline or Polycrystalline Silicon:

Monocrystalline: Silicon is melted and then slowly drawn out inside the shape of a single cylindrical crystal, referred to as a boule.

Polycrystalline: Silicon is melted after which allowed to kick back and solidify in a mold, growing multiple crystals.

3. Slicing Silicon into Wafers:

The silicon block (boule or block) is sliced into very thin wafers the usage of a diamond determined. These wafers characteristic the substrate for the solar cells.

four. Surface Texturing:

The wafers are textured to create a tough surface. This will increase mild absorption, thereby developing the overall performance of the solar cellular.

five. N-Type and P-Type Layer Creation:

In order to generate an electric powered powered present day-day, sun cells are built as PN junctions. This is normally finished with the resource of introducing small portions of numerous materials (doping) into the silicon wafer.

For example, introducing boron will create a incredible (P-kind) layer, at the identical time as introducing phosphorus will create a terrible (N-kind) layer. The junction of these layers is wherein electron motion will arise at the same time as uncovered to daylight hours.

6. Anti-Reflective Coating:

An anti-reflective coating is applied to the silicon wafer to lessen the amount of moderate it's miles contemplated off the floor. This allows growth the quantity of mild absorbed and, therefore, the overall performance of the sun cellular.

7. Electrical Contacts:

Metal contacts are deposited at the top and bottom of the sun cellular to extract the contemporary-day generated at the same time as daylight hours hits the mobile. Typically, the the the front factor has a grid-like sample to permit daylight to however penetrate the mobile, while the lower back is generally genuinely blanketed.

eight. Assembly into Solar Panels:

Individual sun cells are then interconnected (typically in series) and assembled into large panels. The interconnected cells are encapsulated among layers of protecting materials (often glass on the the front, and a polymer-based totally fabric at the lower again).

nine.   Final Module Protection and Framing:

Fig 1.6

To shield solar cells, an prolonged lasting glass layer is delivered, and an encapsulant usually crafted from ethylene-vinyl acetate (EVA) secures the cells of their right function.

The lower back sheet gives insulation and contributes to the overall structural integrity of the panel. Meanwhile, an aluminium frame offers help and makes mounting the panel a whole lot less complicated. The junction discipline houses important electric powered connections and skip diodes, which save you strength loss due to shading

Chapter 13: Off-Grid Solar Systems

2.1 What is an off-grid solar tool?

An off-grid sun device, moreover called a stand-alone energy device (SAPS), is a self-contained electric powered technology and storage device this is certainly independent of the software grid. Off-grid sun systems generate power thru solar panels and shop the strength in batteries to be used as desired, day or night time. They are usually applied in long way flung places, in which connecting to the principle electric powered grid is impractical or too high priced, or through the use of manner of folks that want to collect energy independence and reduce their environmental effect.

Fig 2.1

An off-grid sun system consists of numerous key components that art work collectively to transform sunlight hours into usable energy:

1.   Solar panels: These are the number one power supply for the device. Solar panels,

118

moreover known as photovoltaic (PV) panels, convert sunlight hours into direct contemporary (DC) power. The wide range and period of solar panels preferred rely on the energy requirements of the area and the amount of daylight hours available.

2. Charge controller: The rate controller regulates the flow of strength from the sun panels to the battery economic organization. It ensures that the batteries are charged efficiently and prevents them from overcharging, which could result in decreased battery existence and capacity protection dangers.

three. Battery financial group: The battery monetary organization stores the electricity generated through the sun panels to be used while there may be little or no daylight hours, collectively with in a few unspecified time within the future of cloudy days or at night time. Batteries used in off-grid sun structures are commonly deep-cycle batteries, designed to offer consistent electricity output and resist common charging and discharging.

4. Inverter: Most household home equipment and electronics use alternating contemporary (AC) strength, even as sun panels produce DC energy. The inverter's role is to convert the DC electricity from the sun panels and batteries into AC power that can be used by preferred domestic gadget.

5. Wiring and protection devices: The tool's wiring connects all of the additives, permitting energy to float among them. It is essential to use suitable cables and protection gadgets, along with fuses and circuit breakers, to defend the system from electrical faults and functionality risks.

Off-grid sun systems require careful planning and layout to ensure that they could provide enough energy to fulfill the power desires of the clients. This includes calculating the required sun panel and battery capability, choosing suitable additives, and designing a solar panel array that maximizes electricity technology. Additionally, off-grid solar structures may moreover require more huge interest to energy conservation and overall performance, because of the truth the to be had electricity deliver is confined via the scale of the solar array and battery financial institution.

2.2 Why Go Off-Grid?

Fig 2.2

There are severa reasons why individuals and families pick out to move off-grid and select a stand-on my own strength tool. Some of the maximum not unusual motivations encompass:

Remote area: In frequently, off-grid sun structures are installed in far flung or rural areas wherein connecting to the software program application grid isn't always viable or fee-powerful. Extending energy lines to those locations may be prohibitively costly, making off-grid sun systems a more practical and proper price answer.

Energy independence: By generating and storing their very very own energy, off-grid solar device users can become absolutely self-enough and no longer reliant on software program software companies for their energy desires. This can offer a revel in of freedom and control over energy production and intake.

Environmental impact: Off-grid sun structures harness easy, renewable energy from the solar, reducing the reliance on fossil fuels and lowering greenhouse fuel emissions. For environmentally conscious humans, going off-grid may be an effective manner to reduce their carbon footprint.

Reliability: Off-grid sun systems aren't trouble to power outages and fluctuations which can have an effect at the application grid. By having an unbiased energy deliver, clients can hold a regular and reliable supply of strength, even in the event of natural failures or grid failures.

Cost financial financial savings: While the preliminary investment in an off-grid sun gadget can be large, the lengthy-time period monetary savings can outweigh the costs. Off-grid device customers can avoid monthly software bills and capacity will increase in electricity costs. Additionally, there are often economic incentives and tax credit score to be had for putting in renewable power systems, similarly lowering the overall price.

Scalability and customization: Off-grid sun structures may be designed and scaled to fulfill the particular electricity desires of the customers. This lets in for additonal flexibility and customization in comparison to grid-tied systems, which may be situation to software program organization regulations and rules.

Learning and private increase: Building and maintaining an off-grid sun system may be an educational and profitable revel in. By appealing within the method of designing, putting in, and keeping the device, clients can increase a deeper information of power manufacturing and manage, in addition to precious talents in problem-fixing, resourcefulness, and self-reliance.

Chapter 14: Understanding Electricity Basics

3.1 Basic Electrical Concepts: Voltage, Current, Resistance, and Power

To layout, set up, and preserve an off-grid sun machine, it's miles vital to have a essential knowledge of the fundamental standards of electricity. This section will introduce the center thoughts of voltage, contemporary, resistance, and power.

1.   Voltage (V):

Voltage, measured in volts (V), represents the electric capability distinction amongst factors in a circuit. It is the pressure that pushes electric powered powered charge (in the shape of electrons) thru a conductor, which includes a cord. In a solar device, the voltage output of the sun panels and batteries determines the amount of electrical capability to be had to energy appliances and gadgets.

2.   Current (I):

Current, measured in amperes or amps (A), represents the go along with the drift of electrical fee thru a conductor. It is analogous to the go along with the go along with the glide of water through a pipe; the greater the modern, the more price is being transferred. In a solar device, the cutting-edge is proper now associated with the quantity of energy generated through the solar panels and the strength fed on via the related gadgets.

three. Resistance (R):

Resistance, measured in ohms (Ω), is the opposition to the go together with the glide of electrical present day-day in a conductor or circuit. Resistance reasons some of the electric strength to be converted into warm temperature, that might result in electricity loss. In a solar device, resistance can occur in the wiring, connectors, and various components. Minimizing resistance is critical for maximizing the performance of the tool.

4. Power (P):

Power, measured in watts (W), represents the charge at which electric powered powered power is transformed into unique sorts of power, which incorporates moderate or warmth. It is the made from voltage and present day (P = V x I). In a solar device, power is generated through the sun panels, saved inside the batteries, and consumed thru the associated appliances and devices.

Understanding those smooth electric requirements is critical for the a achievement layout and operation of an off-grid solar device. In the following sections, we are able to find out devices of dimension, clean math for electric powered calculations, and the way those standards are completed in solar device format and sizing.

three.2 Electricity Water Analogy

The voltage, current, and resistance in an electrical circuit can be defined the usage of the water analogy, which compares the flow of electricity to the waft of water through a pipe. This analogy lets in to simplify and visualize the standards for oldsters which may be new to electronics or have problem expertise the ones electric powered parameters.

Fig 3.1

1.   Voltage (Water Pressure)

In the water analogy, voltage can be as compared to water strain. The extra the water stress in a pipe, the greater force it has to push water through the pipe. Similarly, voltage is the force or "electrical strain" that pushes electric powered rate (measured in coulombs) via a conductor or circuit. Voltage is typically measured in volts (V).

2.   Current (Water Flow)

Current is similar to the go with the float of water via a pipe. Just because the water float represents the amount of water passing through the pipe over a time body, the electric cutting-edge represents the quantity of electrical price transferring through a conductor or circuit over a time period.

Current is commonly measured in amperes (A) or amps.

three. Resistance (Pipe Size)

Resistance in an electrical circuit may be in evaluation to the size of the pipe in the water analogy. A pipe with a smaller diameter creates more resistance to water float, making it more tough for water to pass via. Similarly, resistance in a circuit represents the competition or hassle to the float of electrical contemporary. The resistance is predicated upon on elements just like the material of the conductor, its length, and its pass-sectional vicinity. Resistance is normally measured in ohms (Ω).

3.3 Understand Of Ohm's Law

To design, installation, and preserve an off-grid sun machine, it is critical to have a clean understanding of the connection amongst voltage, modern-day-day, resistance, and energy. These fundamental electric powered ideas are interconnected, and their relationship can be expressed thru severa key components.

I. Ohm's Law:

Fig three.2

Ohm's Law describes the relationship between voltage (V), modern-day (I), and resistance (R) in an electrical circuit:

$V = I \times R$

Where:

V is the voltage (in volts)

I is the modern-day (in amperes)

R is the resistance (in ohms)

Ohm's Law can be rearranged to treatment for current-day or resistance:

$I = V / R$

$R = V / I$

The water analogy also can be used to apprehend Ohm's Law, the water drift

130

(current) via a pipe is at once proportional to the water pressure (voltage) and inversely proportional to the dimensions of the pipe (resistance). The more the water stress and the larger the pipe, the more water flows through it. Similarly, a higher voltage and lower resistance in a circuit result in a better electric powered powered current-day flowing through it.

II. Power (P):

Fig three.Three

The electricity in an electrical circuit is the manufactured from voltage (V) and modern (I):

$P = V \times I$

Where:

P is the energy (in watts)

V is the voltage (in volts)

I is the current-day (in amperes)

III. Combining Ohm's Law and Power:

By combining Ohm's Law and the energy equation, we're capable of unique strength in terms of resistance and present day, or voltage and resistance:

$P = I^2 \times R$

$P = V^2 / R$

Relationship among Power, Energy, and Time: Watt-hours and Kilowatt-hours

To layout and duration an off-grid sun device efficaciously, it's far crucial to recognize the relationship among energy, energy, and time. This section will discover how watt-hours and kilowatt-hours are used to symbolize power intake and production in a solar machine.

Fig three.Four

1.   Energy (E): Energy, measured in watt-hours (Wh) or kilowatt-hours (kWh), represents the quantity of electrical energy ate up or generated over the years. It is the made of energy (in watts or kilowatts) and time (in hours).

2.   Watt-hour (Wh): A watt-hour is the amount of strength fed on or generated by using the usage of a tool with a power score of 1 watt walking for one hour. For example, a 60-watt slight bulb working for three hours might also need to devour 100 and 80 watt-hours of power (60 W x 3 h = one hundred eighty Wh).

3.   Kilowatt-hour (kWh): A kilowatt-hour is same to at the least one,000 watt-hours. It is the same vintage unit of measurement for power intake and technology in every grid-tied and rancid-grid structures. For example, if a 1,000-watt appliance operates for two hours, it would devour 2 kilowatt-hours of power (1 kW x 2 h = 2 kWh).

To calculate the power intake of an device or device in watt-hours or kilowatt-hours, use the following components:

E (Wh) = P (W) x t (h)

E (kWh) = P (kW) x t (h)

Where:

E is the energy intake or generation in watt-hours or kilowatt-hours

P is the electricity score of the tool or tool in watts or kilowatts

t is the time for the duration of which the equipment or tool operates, in hours

Understanding the connection among energy, electricity, and time is important for determining the power requirements of your off-grid sun device. By calculating the power intake of each device and device to your tool, you may estimate the complete each day electricity needs and because it have to be period your solar array and battery financial institution.

3.Four. Series and Parallel Connection

Series and parallel connections are processes to arrange electric powered components, which includes resistors, capacitors, or batteries, in a circuit. Each shape of connection has its first rate traits and applications.

Fig 3.Five

Series Connection:

In a chain connection, additives are linked save you-to-cease, forming a single route for the modern to go with the go with the flow. The present day stays the same within the route of the entire path. If one factor fails or is disconnected, the present day will save you flowing through the complete circuit, much like a damage in a sequence.

Characteristics of Series Connection:

The wellknown resistance (R_total) inside the circuit is the sum of the character resistances:

R_total = R1 + R2 + R3 + ...

The common voltage (V_total) throughout the circuit is the sum of the man or woman voltage drops in some unspecified time in the future of each difficulty:

V_total = V1 + V2 + V3 + ...

The cutting-edge (I) flowing via every component is the same.

Series connections are often used at the same time as it is critical for the modern-day to skip via every problem in a selected series or even as a voltage drop for the period of each issue is preferred.

Parallel Connection:

In a parallel connection, additives are associated aspect-via the use of-facet, forming more than one paths for the modern to waft. The voltage at some stage in every path remains the equal. If one component fails or is disconnected, the contemporary-day-day will maintain to drift via the closing paths, much like the go along with the go with the flow of water via a couple of channels.

Characteristics of Parallel Connection:

The reciprocal of the overall resistance (1/R_total) inside the circuit is the sum of the reciprocals of the man or woman resistances:

1/R_total = 1/R1 + 1/R2 + 1/R3 + ...

The everyday modern-day (I_total) flowing through the circuit is the sum of the character currents flowing through every aspect:

I_total = I1 + I2 + I3 + ...

The voltage (V) sooner or later of each element is the same.

Parallel connections are generally used while additives want to feature independently, and a constant voltage is needed during each thing.

three.Five Difference Between AC and DC

Fig three.6

In a solar electricity tool, you can probable have types of electric powered indicators: DC (Direct Current) and AC (Alternating Current). Knowing the versions among the ones indicators will assist you determine out which devices to use, in which to use them, and why they're crucial. Let's spoil it down:

137

DC (Direct Current):

DC is an electrical signal that generally flows in a single path for the duration of the circuit. In a sun electricity system, solar panels generate DC energy when they convert daylight into power. Batteries moreover keep and deliver electricity as DC.

AC (Alternating Current):

AC is an electrical sign that modifications direction to and fro periodically. This is the form of energy we use in our houses to power most of our home device, like fridges, televisions, and computer systems.

You is probably thinking, if AC signal continues converting, how will we degree its fee? Well, on the equal time as we degree AC with equipment like digital multimeters, they show us a completely unique price called the Root Mean Square (RMS). So, with a everyday multimeter, you are normally seeing the RMS charge, till it says in any other case.

RMS, or Root Mean Square (RMS):

138

RMS, is a mathematical manner to represent the "powerful" or "commonplace" price of an AC (alternating modern-day) voltage or modern. Since AC values oscillate among outstanding and lousy, genuinely taking a mean need to result in a rate of zero. Hence, the RMS charge is used to get a large commonplace.

Here's a simplified explanation:

Square all of the right now values of the AC waveform over one whole cycle. Squaring makes all the values excessive fine.

Find the mean (common) of these squared values.

Take the square root of that suggest.

The RMS rate offers a useful degree because it relates directly to the energy or electricity related to the AC waveform. For many purposes, the RMS fee of an AC waveform gives an identical DC (direct contemporary) fee. For example, an AC voltage with an RMS charge of 100 twenty volts will supply the

139

equal amount of electricity to a resistor as a DC voltage of one hundred and twenty volts.

Why Do We Need Both Signals in a Solar Power System?

Solar panels produce DC energy, however most of our household appliances run on AC strength. To make the solar electricity usable for those home system, we need to transform the DC electricity from the sun panels into AC power. That is wherein a device known as an inverter is available in. The inverter takes the DC electricity from the solar panels or batteries and turns it into AC strength for use in your own home.

3.6 Simple Math for Electrical Calculations

In designing and sizing an off-grid solar system, it is critical that allows you to perform fundamental electric calculations to determine tool requirements and components. This segment will introduce a few easy mathematical formula and examples that may be utilized in sun device layout.

1. Calculating Power (P): Power is the made from voltage and modern-day ($P = V \times I$). For example, if an gadget operates at 100 twenty volts and attracts five amps of cutting-edge-day, its strength consumption is 600 watts (one hundred twenty V x 5 A = six hundred W).

2. Calculating Energy Consumption (E): Energy intake is the product of power and time ($E = P \times t$). For example, if a six hundred-watt system operates for three hours, it might eat 1,800 watt-hours of strength (six hundred W x three h = 1,800 Wh).

3. Calculating Total Daily Energy Consumption: To estimate the entire each day electricity consumption of your off-grid solar machine, calculate the energy consumption for each appliance and upload them together. For example:

Appliance A: two hundred W, used for four hours every day = 800 Wh

Appliance B: a hundred W, used for six hours every day = 600 Wh

Appliance C: 50 W, used for eight hours each day = four hundred Wh

Total each day electricity intake = 800 Wh + 600 Wh + four hundred Wh = 1,800 Wh or 1.Eight kWh

4. Calculating Current from Power and Voltage: Using Ohm's Law ($I = V / R$) and the strength equation ($P = V \times I$), we are able to calculate the modern (I) in a circuit at the same time as given the electricity (P) and voltage (V):

$I = P / V$

For example, if an system consumes 600 watts of strength at a voltage of 100 twenty volts, it attracts a modern of five amps (600 W / one hundred and twenty V = 5 A).

five. Calculating Resistance from Voltage and Current: Using Ohm's Law ($R = V / I$), we are able to calculate the resistance (R) in a circuit while given the voltage (V) and cutting-edge (I):

R = V / I

For example, if the voltage throughout a resistor is 12 volts, and the cutting-edge flowing via it's miles 2 amps, the resistance is 6 ohms (12 V / 2 A = 6 Ω).

By making use of those clean mathematical formulation, you may carry out important electric powered calculations to layout and duration your off-grid solar device.

3.7 Energy Cost

Every nation or u.S.A. Of the united states has special charges for energy. To decide how masses, you owe your energy agency for utilization, it's miles important to be privy to your nearby energy fee.

If we take the U.S. National commonplace charge of $zero.12 in keeping with kilowatt-hour for instance and also you run a LED mild bulb with a power rating of 20 Watts for 12 hours every day over a span of 30 days, proper proper right here's the manner to compute the fee:

1. Determine Daily Energy Consumption:

Energy (in watt-hours) = Power (in watts) × Time (in hours)

= 20W x 12h = 240Wh

This way the slight makes use of 240 watt-hours each day.

2. Estimate Monthly Energy Consumption

Monthly Energy (in watt-hours) = Daily Energy (in watt-hours) × Number of days

= 2400Wh×30days = 7200Wh

This is equal to 7200 watt-hours or 7.2 kilowatt-hours (as 1 kilowatt-hour = a thousand watt-hours).

3. Calculate Monthly Cost

You can effortlessly determine how a whole lot; you owe your power company by way of way of the usage of this clean math

Monthly Electricity Bill (in $) = Monthly Energy (in kilowatt-hours) x Electricity Rate (in $/kWh)

= 7.2kWh x $zero.12/kWh = $0.864

So, the usage of a 20-Watt mild for 12 hours every day over 30 days will result in a value of $zero.864.

Chapter 15: Solar Batteries

Off-grid solar structures generate electricity in some unspecified time in the future of the day, but this strength deliver is inconsistent due to versions in daylight due to weather conditions or the day-night time time time cycle. Batteries are essential components in off-grid solar systems due to the reality they deal with the intermittent nature of solar power technology, ensuring a non-stop and reliable supply of strength. By storing more sun strength produced sooner or later of the day, batteries can provide energy for the duration of intervals whilst sun manufacturing is low, such as all through the night or on cloudy days.

The number one function of batteries in off-grid solar structures is to keep electric strength and supply it at the same time as preferred. This power garage capability is essential for maintaining a strong power supply and fending off blackouts or electricity disruptions. Batteries additionally assist in optimizing the use of sun strength by using manner of allowing the machine to maintain surplus energy in some unspecified time in the future of peak production durations and launch it inside the direction of peak intake durations or whilst solar energy production is low.

four.1 Types of Lead Acid Battery

Lead-acid batteries are categorized into fundamental kinds: Flooded Lead-Acid (FLA) and Sealed Lead-Acid (SLA). Each type has its specific production traits, blessings, and disadvantages.

Fig four.1

Source: Exide Battery

Fig four.2

Source: Open Stax

1. Flooded Lead-Acid (FLA) Batteries:

Flooded lead-acid batteries, additionally referred to as wet cellular or vented batteries were the most not unusual sort of lead-acid

147

battery for decades. In the ones batteries, the lead plates are submerged in a liquid electrolyte solution of sulphuric acid and water.

These batteries incorporate liquid electrolyte solution, which incorporates sulfuric acid and water, wherein the lead plates are submerged. The manufacturing of FLA batteries includes exquisite and awful plates crafted from lead dioxide (PbO2) and sponge lead (Pb), respectively, which can be suspended inside the electrolyte answer. To prevent quick circuits, porous separators crafted from substances like rubber, PVC, or microporous polyethylene are positioned the various notable and horrible plates. The battery cells, plates, and electrolyte are housed in a protracted lasting place, usually fabricated from difficult plastic. Each cell has a vent cap that allows gases to get away at a few degree in the charging machine and prevents the ingress of contaminants.

The exploded diagram of flooded lead acid battery is shown under.

Fig 4.Three

Source: Elsevier B.V

Advantages of lead-acid batteries:

Affordability: FLA batteries are generally extra fee-powerful in assessment to distinct battery sorts, making them a popular choice for off-grid sun systems with price range constraints.

Availability: Flooded Lead-acid batteries are broadly available in numerous sizes and capacities, making it clean to find out a appropriate alternative for a particular off-grid sun gadget

Proven normal usual overall performance: With over a century of use in severa programs, lead-acid batteries have a properly-established music report for reliability and everyday overall performance.

Disadvantages of lead-acid batteries

Maintenance: Flooded lead-acid batteries require everyday safety, along with topping up with distilled water and checking electrolyte ranges. This may be time-consuming and may not be appropriate for a long manner off or unattended installations.

Lower energy density: Lead-acid batteries have a lower strength density in contrast to lithium-ion batteries, due to this they require greater vicinity to shop the identical amount of power.

Shorter lifespan: They have a shorter lifespan than lithium-ion batteries, especially at the same time as subjected to deep discharges or excessive temperatures.

Environmental worries: Due to the presence of lead and sulphuric acid, lead-acid batteries should be handled and disposed of carefully to decrease environmental impact.

2. Sealed Lead-Acid (SLA) Batteries:

Sealed Lead-Acid (SLA) batteries are a form of lead-acid battery that has been sealed and designed to be preservation-unfastened. They are an appealing choice for off-grid solar systems, uninterruptible energy materials (UPS), and different programs in which everyday renovation may not be feasible. Sealed Lead-Acid (SLA) batteries also are called VRLA or valve-regulated lead-acid. They have a stress-sensitive valve that robotically controls the emission of gases, but in regular operation situations, they are closed. They are opened robotically to release gases in case there may be excessive strain inside the battery if there may be some factor wrong with the battery, like a short circuit.

SLA batteries are available number one subtypes: Absorbent Glass Mat (AGM) and Gel.

Fig four.Four

Fig four.Five

Source: electricity sonic

Absorbent Glass Mat (AGM) batteries:

151

AGM batteries are constructed with superb and bad plates fabricated from lead dioxide (PbO2) and sponge lead (Pb), similar to Flooded Lead-Acid (FLA) batteries. However, as opposed to a liquid electrolyte, AGM batteries use a specially porous fiberglass separator that absorbs the electrolyte, making the battery spill-evidence and more proof in opposition to vibration. This fiberglass mat permits maintain close to contact the numerous electrolyte and the plates, enhancing the battery's traditional usual overall performance.

Gel Batteries:

Gel batteries additionally characteristic alternating quality and terrible plates product of lead dioxide and sponge lead. The key distinction among Gel batteries and specific lead-acid batteries is the usage of a gel-like electrolyte. The gel electrolyte is created through including silica to the sulphuric acid answer, forming a thick, non-spillable gel that forestalls leakage and lets in the battery to feature in severa orientations.

Advantages of Sealed Lead-Acid (SLA):

Sealed Lead-Acid (SLA) batteries offer numerous blessings over Flooded Lead-Acid (FLA) batteries, making them a famous choice for severa packages, together with off-grid solar structures. Some of the critical detail advantages of SLA batteries over FLA batteries are:

Maintenance-unfastened: SLA batteries are sealed and do now not require normal maintenance responsibilities together with topping up with distilled water or equalization charging. This function makes them a extra reachable desire for applications in which everyday renovation may be difficult or now not viable.

Spill-proof and leak-evidence: Both Absorbent Glass Mat (AGM) and Gel SLA batteries have immobilized electrolytes, which gets rid of the chance of spills or leaks. This feature makes

SLA batteries more secure to apply in various orientations and in situations in which liquid electrolyte spills can also moreover reason harm or pose a chance.

No off-gassing: During the charging way, FLA batteries produce hydrogen and oxygen gases, which can be vented via the battery caps. SLA batteries, however, have a recombination system that stops maximum of the gases from escaping, making them a greater environmentally pleasant choice.

Better wellknown performance in immoderate temperatures: SLA batteries, especially AGM batteries, usually carry out higher in high temperature situations in contrast to FLA batteries, making them suitable to be used in harsh environments.

Lower self-discharge price: SLA batteries have a decrease self-discharge fee in assessment to FLA batteries, letting them hold their rate for extra extended durations when no longer in use. This function makes them pleasant for packages with irregular charging patterns or in which lengthy periods of nation of no hobby are predicted.

Despite the ones advantages, it is important to note that SLA batteries are more highly-priced than Flooded Lead-Acid (FLA) batteries.

4.2 Types of Lithium Battery

Lithium-ion batteries have received reputation in modern-day years because of their superior everyday usual overall performance, higher electricity density, and longer lifespan in comparison to conventional lead-acid batteries. They are increasingly more being utilized in off-grid sun structures, electric powered powered cars, and patron electronics.

Fig 4.6

Source: Greensun Solar

Construction and walking precept

Lithium-ion batteries are composed of a couple of cells that encompass a splendid electrode (cathode), a terrible electrode

155

(anode), an electrolyte, and a separator. The cathode is typically made from lithium steel oxide, on the same time as the anode is crafted from carbon, regularly within the shape of graphite. The electrolyte is a lithium salt solution in an natural solvent, and the separator is a thin porous membrane that maintains the electrodes from touching every unique at the same time as allowing the passage of lithium ions.

Fig 4.7

During the discharge method, lithium ions flow into from the anode to the cathode thru the electrolyte, producing an electric powered powered powered modern-day. When the battery is recharged, lithium ions flow into again from the cathode to the anode.

There are numerous chemistries of lithium-ion batteries, with each imparting unique normal overall performance traits. Some not unusual lithium-ion chemistries embody:

Lithium Iron Phosphate (LiFePO4): LiFePO4 batteries are acknowledged for their lengthy cycle existence, thermal balance, and protection. They are often preferred for solar power garage packages due to their sturdiness and decrease hazard of thermal runaway.

Lithium Cobalt Oxide (LiCoO2): LiCoO2 batteries have a excessive electricity density, making them famous in transportable electronics together with smartphones and laptops. However, they have got decrease thermal stability and are more prone to thermal runaway, making them lots less suitable for large-scale energy storage applications.

Lithium Manganese Oxide (LiMn2O4): LiMn2O4 batteries offer an awesome balance between power density, power output, and safety. They are regularly applied in electricity device and electric automobiles.

Lithium Nickel Manganese Cobalt Oxide (LiNiMnCoO2 or NMC): NMC batteries offer excessive energy density and an extended cycle life, making them appropriate for electric powered powered motors and a few table bound strength garage programs.

4.Three Lithium Iron Phosphate (LiFePO4 or LFP) Batteries

LFP are a type of lithium-ion battery that has received recognition because of their safety, prolonged cycle life, and amazing thermal balance. LFP batteries are appreciably implemented in electric powered powered vehicles, renewable strength systems, and diverse different applications. Here are some information and types of LFP batteries:

LFP batteries have a comparable manufacturing to different lithium-ion batteries, collectively with a incredible electrode (cathode), a horrible electrode (anode), an electrolyte, and a separator. The cathode is made from lithium iron phosphate (LiFePO4), while the anode is typically crafted from carbon, regularly within the shape of graphite. The electrolyte is a lithium salt answer in an natural solvent, and the separator is a thin porous membrane that keeps the electrodes from touching every unique whilst permitting the passage of lithium ions.

During the discharge manner, lithium ions go with the flow from the anode to the cathode thru the electrolyte, generating an electric powered powered modern. When the battery is recharged, lithium ions bypass decrease returned from the cathode to the anode.

Varieties of LFP Batteries:

Lithium Iron Phosphate (LFP) batteries are available in tremendous form elements and types, catering to severa packages and requirements. The important forms of LFP batteries are based on their mobile layout, which incorporates:

Prismatic LFP cells:

Fig four.Eight

Prismatic LFP cells are rectangular-normal cells which might be famous in electric powered automobiles and big-scale energy garage structures because of their immoderate power density and modular layout. Prismatic cells are encased in a difficult aluminum or metallic casing that gives structural help and allows burn up warm temperature for the duration of operation. These cells may be without hassle assembled into battery packs via stacking and connecting them in series or parallel configurations to gain the preferred voltage and potential.

Cylindrical LFP cells:

Fig four.Nine

Cylindrical LFP cells have a cylindrical form and are commonly applied in transportable electronics, electricity system, and smaller-scale energy storage systems. They are available in severa sizes, together with 18650, and 32650, with the numbers indicating the cell's diameter and period in millimetres. Cylindrical cells have a steel or aluminium casing, supplying structural manual and safety.

Pouch LFP cells:

Fig 4.10

Pouch LFP cells characteristic a bendy and lightweight packaging, commonly crafted from laminated aluminum and polymer films. This layout allows pouch cells to be light-weight and occupy a whole lot an awful lot much less vicinity, making them ideal for transportable electronics and electric powered automobiles, wherein weight and location are vital elements. Pouch cells may be assembled into battery packs via stacking and connecting them in series or parallel configurations, and that they often require more aid systems or enclosures to keep their shape and offer protection.

Custom LFP battery packs:

Fig four.Eleven

Custom LFP battery packs are assembled the use of prismatic, cylindrical, or pouch cells to satisfy particular voltage, functionality, and shape detail requirements for numerous programs. Custom battery packs may additionally moreover include integrated battery control structures (BMS), thermal management structures, and safety circuits, making sure the stable and green operation of the battery.

Advantages of LFP Batteries:

Safety: LFP batteries have a extra strong chemistry in evaluation to precise lithium-ion batteries, reducing the risk of thermal runaway and making them a safer preference.

Long cycle lifestyles: LFP batteries usually have an prolonged cycle lifestyles than exclusive lithium-ion chemistries, making them appropriate for packages wherein the battery undergoes frequent charge and discharge cycles.

High thermal stability: LFP batteries can function in a big temperature variety without huge degradation, making them appropriate for use in severa environments.

Environmentally great: LFP batteries do not include poisonous heavy metals like cobalt or nickel, making them a extra environmentally pleasant desire.

Disadvantages of Lithium Batteries:

Cost: Lithium-ion batteries have a propensity to be extra pricey than wonderful types of batteries which include lead-acid. This is due to the high charge of lithium and one-of-a-kind materials used of their production.

Safety Concerns: If improperly handled or charged, lithium-ion batteries can overheat and probable lure fireplace or explode. This is due to a phenomenon referred to as thermal runaway. However, the danger is considerably decrease with Lithium Iron Phosphate (LFP) batteries, which might be considered some of the safest lithium-ion chemistries.

Requires Protection Circuit: Lithium-ion batteries require a protection circuit to save you overcharging or discharging, which could damage the battery and pose safety risks. This adds to the complexity and fee of the battery device.

Sensitivity to High Temperatures: Lithium-ion batteries can degrade quicker if uncovered to high temperatures. This may be a problem in applications or environments wherein excessive temperatures can't be averted.

4.Four Battery State of Charge (SoC)

The u . S . A . Of fee (SoC) is defined as the quantity of energy in a battery, expressed as a percent of the strength stored in a totally charged battery. Discharging a battery outcomes in a lower in state of price, at the same time as charging results in an increase in country of price. If a battery's SoC is 100%, it is completely charged, on the identical time as an SoC of 0% manner it's miles actually discharged.

SoC is generally calculated based totally on the modern output of a battery and its diagnosed ability.

For example, if a battery has a capacity of a hundred ampere-hours (Ah) and it has supplied 20 Ah of modern, its SoC is probably (a hundred-20)/one hundred * a hundred% = 80%.

Below are the complete voltage chart for Flooded Lead Acid (FLA), Sealed Lead Acid (SLA), Lithium Iron Phosphate (LFP) batteries. Please word, the ones are approximate values and can range based totally on numerous factors which encompass the best battery layout, age, temperature, and usage records. Always speak with the manufacturer's specs for correct facts.

Fig four.12

Fig 4.Thirteen

4.Five Battery Depth of Discharge (DoD)

DoD stands for Depth of Discharge and is described as the share of functionality that has been withdrawn from a battery as compared to the general definitely charged capability. By definition, the depth of discharge and u.S. Of america of charge of a battery add to a hundred percent.

It is the opportunity of State of Charge (SoC). If a battery's SoC tells us how lots strength it has left, its DoD tells us how a whole lot it has already used.

Similar to SoC, DoD may be calculated based totally on the cutting-edge output of a battery and its identified functionality. For instance, if a battery has a capability of a hundred ampere-hours (Ah) and it has supplied 20 Ah of cutting-edge, its DoD can be (20/100) * one hundred% = 20%.

DoD and Battery Types:

The appropriate DoD varies between unique varieties of batteries:

166

Lead-acid batteries commonly have a advocated DoD of round 50%. Regularly discharging past this level can significantly reduce their lifespan.

Lithium-ion batteries can typically deal with better DoD levels than lead-acid batteries. Some lithium-ion batteries can be often discharged to a DoD of 80% without drastically impacting their lifespan. Lithium Iron Phosphate (LiFePO4) batteries are frequently rated for 2000 to 5000 cycles at 80% DoD.

4.6 Battery Cycle Life

A single "cycle" for a battery includes discharging the battery from its complete ability proper all the way all the way down to a quality level (Depth of Discharge or DoD), and then recharging it lower returned as lots as entire capability. The cycle life is the variety of those fee-discharge cycles a battery can undergo earlier than its performance degrades to a awesome degree.

The DoD vs Cycle existence curve facilitates in expertise how the lifespan of a battery (measured in cycles) changes with unique depths of discharge.

In modern-day day, a battery's cycle lifestyles decreases because the DoD will boom. This approach that if a battery is regularly discharged deeply (excessive DoD), it is able to not last as many cycles in comparison to even as it is discharged plenty much less deeply (low DoD). This is due to the reality the deeper a battery is discharged in each cycle, the extra put on and tear it reports, primary to a shorter ordinary lifespan.

Fig four.14

Source: gwl-strength

4.7 Battery C Rating

The C rating is described because the rate or discharge cutting-edge divided with the resource of the battery's potential. For instance, if a battery with a ability of one hundred ampere-hours (Ah) is charged or discharged at a price of 50 amperes, its C fee is 50/a hundred = 0.5C.

C ratings are often used to specify each the most stable non-save you discharge rate of a battery and the fee at which it is able to be because it ought to be charged.

The device to calculate C rating is quite trustworthy:

C Rating = Current / Capacity

Where:

Current is the price or discharge modern-day, commonly measured in amperes (A).

Capacity is the battery's capability, generally measured in ampere-hours (Ah).

Fig 4.15

For example, in the above battery with a potential of a hundred Ah is being charged or discharged at a price of 50 A, then its C score is probably:

C Rating = 50 A / 100 Ah = zero.5C

This technique the battery is being charged or discharged at a rate same to 1/2 its functionality constant with hour. If the contemporary had been 100 A as an alternative, the C rating might be 1C, that means the battery is being charged or discharged at a price same to its entire potential in step with hour.

C Rating and Battery Types:

Different styles of batteries can control one-of-a-type C costs:

Lead-acid batteries: These batteries typically determine upon decrease C costs. A commonplace charge fee might be 0.1C to zero.2C, and an normal maximum discharge charge might be 1C to 2C.

Lithium-ion batteries: These batteries can typically address higher C fees than lead-acid batteries. Charge charges of zero.5C to 1C and discharge prices of 1C to 2C are not unusual, notwithstanding the fact that a few sorts can cope with better costs.

C Rating and Battery Life:

The C score can impact the lifespan of a battery. Charging or discharging a battery at a immoderate C charge can purpose it to warmth up, that would boost up potential loss and decrease the battery's lifespan. Therefore, it's also better for the battery's sturdiness to charge and discharge it at decrease C charges.

Fig 4.Sixteen

Chapter 16: Solar Panels

Five.1 what is a Solar Panel?

A solar panel, additionally known as a photovoltaic (PV) module, is a tool that converts daylight into power using a manner known as the photovoltaic effect.

The conventional sun panel includes person sun cells, each of it actually is generally composed of layers of silicon – one layer is doped with impurities to create an additional of electrons (called an n-kind layer), whilst the opportunity layer is doped to create a deficit of electrons (called a p-type layer). When those layers are introduced together, an electric powered region is customary at the junction between them, developing an area known as the depletion place.

Fig five.1

Source: predication

When daylight, composed of particles called photons, hits the solar cell, some photons are absorbed via the semiconductor cloth. The strength from these absorbed photons is transferred to the electrons within the silicon atoms, inflicting them to interrupt unfastened from their atomic bonds. These unfastened electrons are then driven thru the electrical location closer to the n-type layer, at the same time as the "holes" they leave within the decrease back of include pushed toward the p-type layer.

By attaching metal contacts to each layers of the sun cellular, an outdoor electric powered

powered circuit is created. When the loose electrons glide thru this circuit, an electric modern is generated.

five.2 Solar Spectrum Overview

The mild spectrum plays a massive characteristic of their normal overall performance and basic performance. Sunlight consists of some of wavelengths that make up the sun spectrum, together with ultraviolet (UV) moderate, visible moderate, and infrared (IR) light. Each wavelength of light includes a particular quantity of strength, with shorter wavelengths (UV) having extra power than longer wavelengths (IR).

Semiconductor substances in the solar cells can absorb photons at some point of various wavelengths. The absorbed photons switch their strength to the electrons within the semiconductor atoms. The power required to excite an electron and generate energy is referred to as the bandgap energy. The performance of a sun panel is based upon on its functionality to take in and convert photons with specific energies. Ideally, a sun panel must soak up photons with energies identical to or extra than the bandgap strength. However, photons with higher energy than the bandgap energy can create excess warm temperature, reducing the sun panel's overall performance, while photons with lower strength than the bandgap power aren't absorbed and do not contribute to electricity era.

Chapter 17: Earthling And Lightning Protection

Solar installations, like numerous electric structures, require complete protection measures to protect every the tool and the humans the use of it. Among the ones protection measures, earthing (grounding) and lightning protection hold tremendous roles These financial disaster ambitions to make clear those crucial topics, imparting practical insights to manual you via the hows and whys of enforcing effective earthing and lightning safety structures.

10.1 What is Earthing (Grounding)?

Earthing, or grounding, is the exercise of connecting electric systems right away to the earth using conductive substances. This serves to make certain that within the occasion of a fault or surge, extra electrical strength has a steady route to circulate the earth, minimizing the hazard of electrical wonder or fireside.

10.2 Why is Earthing Important?

Imagine your off-grid sun setup as a mini power station. You've have been given some of those cables, devices, and panels generating and transmitting power. With those varieties of additives, topics can without problem pass sideways, and that is wherein grounding is available in as your unsung hero. So, allow's ruin down why you must care:

1.   Personnel Safety

One of the number one reasons for earthing is to protect humans from electric powered shocks. An ungrounded device can turn out to be a dangerous voltage supply if a stay twine comes into touch with a non-electric element, much like the metal frame of a solar panel or an device casing. By grounding those elements, any stray electric electricity is thoroughly channeled into the earth, lowering the hazard of electrical marvel to those interacting with the tool.

2.   Equipment Protection

Electrical surges or spikes can arise for numerous reasons, which encompass lightning moves or malfunctions in electric powered powered components. These surges can damage touchy electronics and unique home device linked to the machine. Grounding offers an possibility course for immoderate electric powered power, diverting it efficaciously into the earth and thereby protective your system.

three. Voltage Stabilization

Grounding guarantees that every one elements of the electric circuit are at the same voltage diploma, relative to the earth. This uniform voltage is vital for the right operation of electrical and virtual devices, contributing to their sturdiness and reliability. It additionally aids in preventing voltage fluctuations that would otherwise purpose intermittent operation or failure of devices.

four. Fault Clearance

A nicely-grounded device lets in the proper operation of overcurrent gadgets like fuses and circuit breakers. When a fault takes place, grounding allows to ensure that sufficient current-day flows to "adventure" those shielding devices, lowering off the electric deliver and thereby stopping further harm or harm.

5.   Electromagnetic Interference

Grounding can reduce the electromagnetic interference (EMI) for your tool. EMI can disrupt the proper functioning of touchy electronics and records lines. A right grounding scheme can act as a protect, supplying a few degree of protection closer to EMI.

6.   Legal Requirements

Finally, right grounding is regularly no longer handiest a remarkable workout but a prison requirement as properly. Electrical codes in loads of jurisdictions mandate grounding for protection motives, and failure to comply can result in fines, prison repercussions, and voided insurance suggestions.

10.Three Two Types of Grounding

There are kinds of grounding: chassis (or mechanical) and electric powered. Both are completely tremendous grounds and ought to be understood efficiently. 'Ground' is only a reference thing; it does not usually advise unbiased.

Setting up correct chassis and electric powered grounds is essential for protection, usual performance, and the sturdiness of structures. Chassis grounds be part of all uncovered steel factors that do not bring contemporary (just like the sun module body, battery case, lower back plate, and mounting structures) collectively and to the floor. This is especially completed for safety. It ensures that if there may be a boom of electrical functionality on any metallic difficulty, it is able to no longer offer you with a surprise when touched. Keep in thoughts, voltage is basically the difference in functionality among points. Properly grounding your device negates this difference, making sure safety

10.Four Key Components to Ground in an Off-Grid Solar System

Fig 10.1

1.   Solar Panels: The metal frames of all sun panels need to be grounded to make certain that they do now not supply a unstable voltage if a fault happens.

2.   Inverter: Inverters should be grounded to make certain protection and right functioning.

three. Racking/Mounting Equipment: The steel additives of your racking system must moreover be grounded.

four.   Battery Bank: Particularly if you're the usage of metal-encased batteries.

10.5 Typical Grounding Method for Mobile Setups

For off-grid cellular setups, which encompass vehicles or boats, it's miles important to hyperlink all metal components to the number one grounding point. This consists of the boat's out of doors hull or a van's essential metallic structure. When putting in this hyperlink in cars, prioritize connecting to the strong structural frame over the flimsier issue panels. Prepare the relationship element by means of using using sanding away any paint, then bore a hollow to attach a cord to the crucial grounding bar. Subsequently, fasten every other wire from this bar to the battery financial institution's number one terrible terminal.

The ground wire want to in form the diameter of its corresponding lively twine. However, producers can also have varying specs in this mission be counted. It's virtually beneficial to searching for recommendation from the consumer manuals of each the charge controller and the inverter to ensure accurate wire sizing.

10.6 Lightning Protection

Lightning is a not unusual motive of disasters in sun photovoltaic (PV) structures. A adverse surge can rise up from lightning that strikes an extended distance from the tool, or maybe among clouds. But most lightning damage is preventable. A lightning safety tool usually includes a aggregate of lightning rods, conductors, and ground electrodes designed to shield a shape and its contents from damage because of electric surges.

Below are the most factors of a widespread lightning protection gadget:

1.   Air Terminals (Lightning Rods)

Air terminals, generally called lightning rods, are metal devices set up at the very nice factors of a shape. Generally crafted from conductive substances which includes copper or aluminum, the ones rods characteristic to draw and seize the electrical discharge from a lightning strike.

2.   Conductors

Conductors are essentially the electrical pathways that facilitate the routing of electrical electricity from the air terminals to the floor rods. These are often robust wires crafted from substances that provide low electric powered resistance, typically copper or aluminum.

3.   Grounding Electrodes (Ground Rods)

The grounding electrodes, or ground rods, are cylindrical rods embedded into the earth. Their primary function is to expend the electric power absorbed through the air terminals into the ground. These rods are normally constructed from quite conductive materials like copper or galvanized steel.

four.   Bonding

Bonding is a vital element of a complete lightning protection technique. This consists of the interconnection of all metal objects in close to proximity to the air terminals and conductors. The motive of bonding is to limit the risk of component flashes, which might be secondary lightning strikes that occur at the same time as the electric discharge seeks opportunity pathways to the ground.

5.   Surge Protection Device (SPD)

Fig 10.2

Fig 10.Three

Surge Protection Device (SPD) is used to guard the gadget's electric powered tool from capability harm because of electric surges or spikes, which may be resulting from way of factors together with lightning movements or energy surges on the grid.